KILIMANJARO
MY STORY

BY

ROD WOOD

I would like to dedicate this book to my son, Richard, for all his support over the years, and to all those who have sought an answer to their life's problems. Reach for the sky!

CONTENTS

1. PREFACE

On June 27th 2012, I left these shores to try and climb Mount Kilimanjaro in Tanzania, the highest mountain in the continent of Africa at 5895 metres above sea level. This had been a lifelong ambition I had hoped to achieve by the time I was fifty years old. That passed me by, but the time had come to turn dreams into reality.

This is my account of the trip, the plans to arrange it all, my training to undertake this adventure, and most importantly the effect it had on me as a person, the highs and lows. But essentially, it is my story and if I seem to waffle a bit in places, I won't apologise because I wanted to put down in words what I felt, saw, and did.

Though undertaken by myself, I received a lot of support from a lot of people both in encouragement and in sponsorship, as I also tried to raise money for Severn Hospice, so they may gain from my achievements as well, if successful.

There were ups and downs, both in the planning and on the walk/climb, but in writing this at least I can savour the memories in what was a once in a lifetime experience. If other people benefit from my words, so be it and I am pleased, but this basically is for me.

If finally getting round to climbing, or trying to climb the mountain took longer than expected, then it would also be true to say that getting round to writing this account has also taken longer than anticipated, but after several attempts and not getting very far, I have at last found the drive to try and complete this, as I write this in early 2015. The memories are still strong but even on the trip, there were times when it was hard to remember every detail, whether through tiredness, or just the awe-inspiring scenery that was around me.

Here goes then, my story!

*

A lifetime ambition of mine ever since I was a teenager had been to stand on the roof of Africa, to climb Mount Kilimanjaro, the highest point in the whole continent of Africa. If my initial aim was to have achieved this by the age of fifty, that passed me by. But the chance did at last come and on July 4th 2012, I finally achieved this goal in my life. If this is only for my own eyes, it is important to me to put this account of my trip, my thoughts and lasting impressions, down on paper as a memoir to me of what I achieved for myself.

As a child, probably when ten or so years old, my initial interest in Africa, and especially East Africa arose. I have recently found an book that I was given on my eleventh birthday by my parents, *Animals of East Africa* by C. A. Spinage, a description and photographs of the animals of this region; quite an advanced book for one of my age then, but the interest was there. At that time, my father's brother, John, had lived in (as was then) Rhodesia for several years. My grandmother had visited on occasions and returned to relate her tales of colonial states, the peoples who lived there, but little of the geography and wildlife of the area.

At my secondary school, Abingdon, during the school holidays we were given a book to read, and after my first term the chosen book by my Form Master, also a Rhodesian, was *Born Free*, the tale of an orphan lion, Elsa, who became quite a celebrity. This as it turned out was the only one of these books that ever captured my imagination, as it was the only one I ever won a prize for. What it did do was introduce me to East Africa, the Game Parks and to some extent, conservation. *Born Free* led onto *Living Free*, *Forever Free*, *The Orphans of Tsavo* and more detailed books on the great Rift Valley and the animal inhabitants there, an interest I have never lost, and if these days I watch very little television, I will always make the effort if it covers the diminishing animal populations of this great continent. I suppose at this stage of my school career, I had decided to become a Zoologist to pursue this interest, but later changed direction to become the Veterinary Surgeon I am today.

My interest in the continent continued though, as I tried to teach myself the geography of the East African region, the makings of the Rift Valley, and the plains that make the Game Reserves. In learning some of the physical geography of the area, Kilimanjaro became known to me, a mountain, an extinct volcano, "THE ROOF of AFRICA". At that stage, though I was not intimate with foreign travel, little was reported of ascents. It certainly had nowhere near the popularity and challenge that it has today, not the thriving hub of the Tanzanian tourist industry. And in those days it was known as Tanganyika. But despite this, somewhere in my mind I created the desire that I wanted to stand on top of this mountain, and because I was there, I would have visited those areas, the Serengeti, Ngorongoro Crater and their wildlife that had so interested me in my teenage years. Then, as my education at school drew to an end, I studied Biology for A-

Level, and we touched on evolution, and the origins of man. This is an area rich in finds of the early humanoids, the excavations of the Leakeys in the Olduvai Gorge. Chapters of real note in how we became what we are today.

And as stated earlier, as this seed was planted, the desire was to do this before I was fifty. School went to university, a degree (and we did get to see some wildlife when sick animals from Clifton Zoo were brought into Langford for treatment, the occasional big cat, zebra), and life went the way of most graduates of that era, no gap years, just straight into your first job, with dreams for the future.

If Africa went more to the back of my mind, with work and hockey taking over, it was certainly never forgotten, with every effort made to follow stories, films, documentaries, whatever there may have been on this area. Political troubles perhaps made it all seem a bit more remote but the fascination continued. And I have surprised myself in not mentioning elephants yet, but the desire remained that at some stage I would see them in their natural environment, and to do that I needed to go to Africa. Other areas boast these wonderful animals, throughout the east and south of the continent, the well-known game reserves of Kruger, the Okavango Delta in the south west, all wonderful places, but it was Tanzania and Kenya that I really wanted to see.

If there was a seed of a plan in my mind some time before, it would have been a three-week trip, one seeing the reserves and their inhabitants, one climbing the mountain, and finally a few days on the East African coast, recuperating and relaxing. Time, political pressures and probably most important, finances, knocked that idea on the head, so the plan looked more like just the mountain.

I wonder how many people would have gone before me if I had undertaken this trek when the idea was first implanted in my mind.

Now, it is a popular expedition, and undertaken by many as

a form of raising money for charity, and some who just want to climb it. Most recently was the climb for Comic Relief undertaken by several celebrities.

As I have already said, Kilimanjaro is the highest mountain in Africa, at 5895 metres, the "roof of Africa", and the highest free-standing mountain (i.e. is not part of a range) in the world. Arising some eighty miles to the eastern side of the plains of the Rift Valley, the three peaks of Meru, Kibo, and Mawenzi (the latter two making up Kilimanjaro) stand proud above the surrounding lands. Kilimanjaro is just south of the Kenyan border in north-west Tanzania, and has become a serious tourist attraction and source of income to this region. It now has its own airport as well to get all the climbers to the mountain in the easiest way.

The origins of the name of the mountain seem a little unclear, with no clear indication whether the word comes from Swahili, Chagga, or Masai, but certainly the highest point, Uhuru, is Swahili for freedom, and obtained its name after independence in 1961.

The mountain goes through several distinct geographical regions of rainforest, heath and moorland, highland desert and the ice fields at the summit. Kilimanjaro is a volcano (though it has been many, many years since an eruption), and around the perimeter of the crater are many ice fields, glaciers, and within the crater itself, the Ash Pit – its mouth. A fascinating mountain, and one which is just at the limits of climbing without artificial breathing equipment.

One should just mention the climate here, as this did have some bearing on the timing of my trip, especially as I really do not do cold, and definitely not cold and wet. The weather at any time of year can be erratic due to the effect the mountain has on wind currents. There are two rainy seasons, and two dry seasons, these being December to March, and then July to early October, and these are generally the chosen times to climb. The dry spell at the start of the year is generally warm, while in the July period it tends to be a bit cooler. The hottest months are January, February, and September. Climbing Kilimanjaro in the two rainy seasons can be less pleasant, thick clouds often shrouding the mountain, with heavy downpours on the lower slopes which can turn into snow higher up. The long rain (masika) is from April to June, the short rain (mvuli) in November and December.

Temperatures can vary wildly from 30°C at the foot of the mountain, plunging to below -20°C on the summit, plus an added wind chill factor which can make it feel colder still. Rainfall is heaviest, and most sustained, in the forests on the south side of the mountain. The least rain falls on the summit.

Whatever the season, the best weather is generally to be had in the morning, with cloud cover building up during the day. However, by evening the skies have generally cleared again.

Obviously like me, a lot of people choose July time, as it is the time of our summer holidays. If this will coincide with a full moon for the final summit climb, this is perfect to give a bit more light for the final climb during the night.

There are six regular ascent routes up the mountain varying in length of time for the climb, distance and grade of difficulty of the climb. They have their own routes to the summit, and then descent routes as well, though these are shared.

Marangu: a 65km, five-day climb, graded as moderate to hard, but a tedious summit route.

Umbwe: a 44km, five-day climb and classed as hard, climbing through the Barranco Valley, and Southern Ice Fields.

Machame: a 61km, five-day climb, and classed as hard, with stunning scenery on the way.

Lemosho: a 72km, seven-day walk, moderate to hard, and with interesting scenery across the Shira Plateau and Southern Ice Fields.

Shira: a 67km, six-day walk, moderate to hard, with no forest section.

Rongai: a 54km, six-day climb, moderate to hard, providing excellent access to Mawenzi, but again a tedious summit climb, and it can be a crowded descent down.

They all offer their different challenges, and with different tour companies offering different ones.

2. THE DECISION IS MADE
DECEMBER 2011

If my life had drifted for a few years, many years, through what I would consider to be an unhappy marriage and never having the relationship with my children I would have hoped for, especially with my daughter, there had seemed little direction in where I was going in my personal life and my career. Though committed to the fact that I would now only be a farm vet until my retirement, I had worked in two partnerships where it would only be fair to say that all involved seemed to be pulling in different directions, and so to me the results of what could have been good businesses were never achieved. And so, after a few years in mixed practice, I now found myself working again solely as a farm vet, though in the area I had worked during the Foot and Mouth outbreak in 2001. That in itself brought back to me many distressing memories involving the wholesale and in my view, an unnecessary destruction of a lot of healthy farm animals, and the mental affects it had had on their owners. So, although I was now again doing the part of veterinary work where my heart was, and working for some wonderful farmers, forward thinking and responsive to advice, there were seeds of self-doubt in my mind.

Foot and Mouth, and the final throes of my marriage occurred roughly at the same time, perhaps the mental anguish of the outbreak on me, hurrying the process of deciding my life needed to change, and that now was the time to go.

Another relationship, wonderful to start with but then turning into a disaster area, partly due to my own doing, and in this time a change of job, moving to where I am now, everything was building towards personal meltdown. It took a lot out of me to get away from that relationship, perhaps a sense of responsibility, but I let it drag on far too long and mainly to my own cost and well-being. Oh, with the knowledge of hindsight!

To get away, I started to go down to Exmoor more frequently and explore parts I had not seen before, even though my parents had been down there thirty-odd years in different places. An enjoyment of walking was developing and it became a great way to spend time especially with Dad as he showed me parts of the Moor he used to trek over when he and Mum had the horses, way off the beaten track, inaccessible to cars.

My friendships over the years hadn't changed. I had never asked or expected people to take sides in the breakdown of my marriage, had never said a bad word about my ex-wife, and so hoped the friendships would carry on from both sides. But that required effort from us both, and I hope, I know, that I have benefitted from that effort to maintain some life-lasting relationships, and can only thank all those involved for the support they have given me over the years, in good times and in bad.

So, it was after one of these trips to Exmoor that I had raced back to Telford one Saturday afternoon to meet up with my mate, Dave Butler and his partner to go to a dinner dance (have always been one for dressing up as in a DJ if the opportunity arose). We were to be accompanied by another of his colleagues from work to make up the party. A lovely lady called Lindsay, whom I had never met before, was quiet to start with but as the evening progressed came more out of herself and was really fun to be with (though this wasn't a blind date). After the disasters of my last relationship I wasn't really looking for another, and as it transpired Lindsay was in a similar position, but over the coming days and weeks, we got to know each other better, had a lot in common, and though holidaying separately at different times, became an integral part of each other's lives. This isn't the place to write about our times together other than to say what wonderful times they were, and our little sojourn to Paris for a long Valentine's break would rate as one of my happiest memories ever. Alas for reasons that I don't still fully understand, all good things come to an end and with the parting of my soulmate, life had taken another step backwards.

And so all the seeds had been sown for an ever-descending spiral, and in the summer of 2010 I was diagnosed with clinical depression. I kept this largely to myself for a long while, on the basis only I could solve it, but where do you start? Everywhere I turned seemed to lead me up a blind alley. I can only reiterate the support of friends at this time, mainly Dave and Anthony Ward, who understood the problem. The kids found it hard to cope with the fact that Dad had a "mental illness", or that's how it seemed to me anyway.

It all created problems at work and I seemed to be falling, falling. My doctor tried various tablets, some with not very pleasant side effects that I soon stopped taking, others didn't seem to make any difference to me at all. I had become a loner, never went out, and couldn't concentrate on anything. The times I took myself to Old Trafford, after twenty minutes or so I would be thinking, *What am I doing here?* But that was the only time I got to spend much time with Lydia, my daughter. So, all in all I couldn't get much enjoyment out of life.

I was one day, late in that year, on a farm doing some work, and on completion was invited in for a cup of tea. I didn't really know Malcolm that well, except that his marriage had recently broken up, but over that cuppa he chatted, thought I hadn't been myself for some time and after much conversation, he thought I shouldn't be sitting in by myself all the time and needed to get out again. He belonged to a singles group and their Christmas party was approaching, so he would take me along as his guest, if I let him know. After much deliberation, I did decide to go, although, I didn't really want to, if for no other reason than just to get out. So on a snowy evening I set off to Oswestry. It was quite fun and afterwards I would have to make the decision whether to join or not. Again, just for the sake of getting out after a few weeks, I decided I would, but on speaking to Malcolm he had found another singles group; we would go along to this group, and see what they were like, as the other was more than a bit staid.

So in February 2011, I went along, very apprehensive, and very unsure of myself. In busy annexe in a pub, a lot of people gathered for this group, Serendipity. I was introduced to one or two, especially the organiser, Margaret, a very welcoming lady. Davina, (there seemed) lots of Susans, Helen (a golfer), and others. These meetings were held every Tuesday and it was the following week when about to depart, I met Jayne, who made a beeline for me. Again, I don't think, well, I knew I wasn't ready for a relationship, but we started going out. The Nile cruise followed and a lot of fun was had, but through all that time I never really felt that now was the time to be with someone. Again, perhaps the wrong time.

During this time, in discussions with my doctor, we had decided that medication for depression was going nowhere so the next course of action would be to try counselling. I was sceptical, being a person who always kept things to myself, and openly doubted that I would open up to a stranger. I was given a referral and after a few weeks this was arranged – a course of eight sessions. At first these seemed to me to be going nowhere, but I persevered. I suppose a negative attitude was almost telling me I didn't want it to work.

Halfway through the sessions, the Nile cruise took place, and here at last was a positive light on the horizon. It was a wonderful holiday, fun, cultured, friendly people, but the turning point was when stumbling across a few lines when reading the ship's physio's brochure.

A few words, but didn't they put everything into perspective for me:

Life is only travelled once
Today's moments become
Tomorrows
Memory
Enjoy
Every moment
Good or bad
Because
The Gift of Life
IS
Life Itself

So, I wasn't going to get anywhere moping, feeling sorry for myself, and if anything was going to happen in my life it was up to me to initiate it. And so, almost at once there was some direction as I saw some order in what I did.

I wasn't happy in my relationship, and one night at Serendipity, Margaret sensed this and asked me if I wanted to have a drink one night to have a chat about things. So we arranged an evening to go, a relaxed and informal evening chatting over a beer (well, not her). I think I had already made up my mind about ending the relationship, but was happy to let it drift along a bit longer. But after our conversation had progressed, it was obvious I was only delaying the inevitable, so the sooner the better (which was the scenario that soon followed, but enough on that).

Conversation got onto other aspects of life and indeed Margaret was much travelled, and so the talk slowly got round to that missed ambition of climbing to the roof of Africa by the time I was fifty. "So why not now?" she said. "It's something you really want to do so what is stopping you?" We talked on this topic for some time, very much me coming up with excuses for not doing it (a reflection of the negativity that had crept into my mind) and her coming up with a counter argument that I should still do it. Eventually the topic of conversation changed onto other things. It was an enjoyable evening so we decided to do it again, trying to point me in the right direction.

And so in early December, we met again, chatted generally, and after a bit came back onto the subject of my mountain. Lo and behold, as if by magic, out of her bag came brochures of walking tours in the world, with the corners of the pages turned over for treks up Kilimanjaro. Again, the reasons I couldn't do it in 2012 – too soon etc., etc., but a bandwagon was starting to roll, and it seemed forces outside my control were pushing me in that direction. And so from that evening the plan was being put in motion. I agreed to look through the brochures, and most importantly would have a medical as there was no point planning if I wasn't medically fit. Margaret had got me these brochures and the name of a travel agent she had used several times for her trips, one that she thought would be worth a try as they had always been very efficient in arrangements for her.

At this time of year, just before Christmas, I have always taken a trip down to Exmoor to see my parents and then on down to Graham's in the little village of Stokeinteignhead, between Shaldon and Torquay. Having departed my parents' and reaching Graham's, it was a beautiful sunny day, exceptional for this time of year. We decided that we would take the dog for a walk just before lunch and set off out of the village, up the valley towards the coast via bridle paths, across fields, crossing the main coast road and reaching the fields nearing the cliffs. We chatted about life in general but, I don't know why, as we reached the cliffs the conversation had changed to Kilimanjaro. I mentioned the conversations with Margaret and that it looked like I may be giving it a go, though to be honest was still looking for excuses not to. My worry, being a poor sleeper, was, could I climb a mountain on a trek of a few days on no sleep? We chatted for some time on the subject, but again saying the next step was a medical, and we would see where we would go from there. A nice chat with a very close and long-term friend who probably knows me as well as anyone does, we arrived back at his house for lunch and an enjoyable few days before departing back to Telford. There was the exchange of Christmas presents before we parted.

Christmas arrived and I opened my presents. From Graham, a guide to climbing Kilimanjaro. Why now, when I had talked about it all these years? It really did seem that the gods had decreed that this was the time.

3. THE PLANNING BEGINS
JANUARY 2012

And so 2012 had begun and the plan needed to be started, but the first step had to be: was I fit enough?

I have always been a keen athlete, hockey and cross country at school, and hockey during my adult life until it got too difficult with my work commitments to carry on playing. So the gym took over, step aerobics, working out myself, circuit training (which I enjoyed enormously, competing against myself, pushing myself to the limit) and running on a treadmill. But over that time I had sustained a few injuries, most worryingly for the trip was a toe injury I had got when running when I was 17 years old. Tripping over an exposed tree root, I had damaged the cartilage in my left big toe, leading to arthritis and at that time, the medical profession had considered shortening the toe to ease the problem. It had settled down, I wouldn't have considered the surgery as it would have curtailed my sports, but of late I had had a few niggles in what was a slightly enlarged joint. I had also sustained a bad knee injury on the right playing hockey at university, which had caused aches on and off since. Both these injuries may cause problems on a prolonged climb and long walk.

And of course I was not getting any younger so, heart, lungs, and blood pressure needed to be checked out. And so as I entered the new year, the first thing to do was to arrange an appointment with my G.P. Dr Underwood, who had helped me through my depression, to see if my body was up to the task – no point going any further if it was not.

I've always found him to be the best doctor I have had,

and so the consultation was informal as he checked me over, and I relayed my concerns. Basically everything was okay, but it had to be up to me how much pain or discomfort I could tolerate to do the walk. The decision then had to be mine, I was fit enough and had to decide for myself. It was getting to the stage where whatever excuse I came up with in my mind a counter argument would nullify my worries. There was no turning away from the fact that the trip was going to go on. Suitable footwear would be beneficial, good advice there. And of course, going to a tropical country, there would be vaccinations to consider. Dr Underwood said he would research my needs, and admitted himself that he quite envied me for doing the trip. He would ring me with the results of his enquiries. I had done some preliminary research into it, but was pretty certain whatever jabs I had had in the past, except perhaps tetanus, had expired. The biggest uncertainty seemed to be over the possibility of vaccination against yellow fever. Some papers say it is essential, certainly if you have entered Tanzania via Kenya, others said it was not necessary anymore. To this day, I am still not sure whether it was necessary but I opted to have it.

The other consideration was malaria, and several people I had spoken to had had bad reactions to anti-malarial drugs, or their side effects. Base camp and the mountain climb were above mosquito level, which I was told the limit was about 1800 metres, but there were the bits in between and it only needs one bite. Addis Ababa and the airport were the risk places, brief visits but a risk nonetheless. Was the risk worth taking? Probably not so, and there was another thing that needed researching by my G.P., and he would let me know when he had found this out. This was lastly altitude sickness, the need for pills, again necessary or not, and again differing reports on their side effects.

The beginning of 2012 therefore had me in a position where having made the decision to go, I needed to organise the travel plans, sort out the medical side which I have touched on above, but will come back to later, and to decide what training I needed to do, how fit to get, and some sort of timescale as to what I would do.

First, my thoughts on the trip. Over the years, as articles appeared in the travel section of the *Daily Telegraph*, I would gloss over them with a passing interest, probably file them away somewhere only to throw them away at a later date in the interests of clutter, but would then go online to find out prices, and other details. Never though, up to this point, with the firm plan that I was going to act on this information. I also didn't know anyone who had done the trip to find out more about it, a good travel firm, route, etc. (other than Kevin just before Christmas, who hated it so much he couldn't offer anything positive). It is surprising now, nearly three years on, how many people I have met who have either done Kili or want to do it.

When I had been talking to Margaret, and encouraged by her to take on this venture, she had given me a couple of travel brochures for this sort of trip. She is a well-travelled lady, and had gone on several of these types of holidays in the past (and still does), covering a wide range of global holidays, but in each brochure there were only a few pages on treks in East Africa, the Game Parks, Kilimanjaro, and combinations of climbs and game reserves. She, in the past, had used a firm called Explore! She had also used a travel agents in Shrewsbury, Peake's Travel, a name that I had forgotten as Lindsay had also used them to arrange one of our trips away. Margaret had suggested that I try them to see what was available, and that they would be very good at arranging everything for me.

And so in early February I took myself into Shrewsbury on an afternoon off, to find out what trips were available, and when. It was obvious when I was at Peake's Travel that this wasn't the most popular holiday destination asked for, if anyone had actually ever asked to go there through this agent! The young lady I spoke to was very helpful, pulling off various bits of information from the web, and finding one or two brochures on Kilimanjaro climbs, including the most up to date 2012 Explore one. I suppose my preference on time was always going to be the two weeks in summer. I have always favoured, end of June/beginning of July, and those dates fitted in with Explore's schedule, as they were also going there just after that, and possibly (but not confirmed yet), the two weeks (actually twelve days, flying out on a Wednesday, returning Sunday morning). A quick breeze through vaccinations, visa requirements and a rough idea of cost, all gave me food for thought to go away and decide what my plans would be.

So I returned home, brochures in hand, to look at and decide what I wanted to do. The available trips through Explore were the Lemosho route and the Rongai route, and looking at the calendar it showed a full moon just after the start of July, ideal for the final ascent in the dark, at least giving some light. Checking with work when I could book my holiday, all these dates were free. Lemosho would give me more time to acclimatise to the altitude on the mountain, and sounded generally a nicer "holiday", not just a quick up and down. June 27th to July 8th therefore was what I would go for, Lemosho, decision made.

Nearing the end of February, I took myself back into Peake's Travel to book it all. The owner, Frances, dealt with me this time, efficiently contacting Explore about availability (no other takers on that trip yet), booking this, and finding out other information that would be of use. I would need a visa to get into Tanzania, and that would either mean going to the embassy in London, or Peake could take care of it all for me. I would need to get my passport to them so they could send it off. A deposit was paid, and the wheels were now in motion for me to go. Exciting stuff, and a lot of interest from Frances, as she had not organised this for anyone before.

Therefore on February 24th, all was starting to happen.

The visa cost was £38 + £35 service charge for the company that Peake's used, as the passport had to be handed in to the embassy in person. The cost of the package for the trip was just over £2200, but that covered flights, entry into Kilimanjaro National Park, hotel and outfitter fees. That would just leave tips for the porters, medical fees, spending money, plus any equipment I would need to acquire.

That was everything just about done in terms of organisation. The passport was duly despatched, and returned with visa, and in May the balance of the holiday was paid. There was one hiccup at the end of April, when having just completed a job on a farm, and reaching the end of the farm drive, my car died. After RAC rescued me and towed me off to the garage, the alternator was diagnosed as the problem, a replacement costing in the order of £800. It was necessary as the car was going nowhere without one, but to this day I think I was stung by the garage, the RAC man suggesting it should cost about £300. This was more than I could afford, and did make me seriously think whether I could afford this holiday, but after much thought I decided to go ahead with it.

There was a slight change in flight times made, but nothing that significant, and as I was later to find out, the tour operators nearly cancelled the whole thing as too few people had taken up these dates.

Holiday insurance had to be dealt with. I thought I was covered through my bank account, but funnily enough their cover finished at 5500 metres, how they wriggle out of these things. Therefore I had to organise special insurance through a company called Insureandgo, who would extend their cover to the altitude I would be reaching.

With all this now sorted out, on collection of my documents, Frances wished me luck, and said to pop in on my return to let her know how it all went so she could share my experiences with anyone else in the future who may want to undertake this trip.

The medical side. I saw Dr Underwood again in the spring and sorted out my vaccinations and prescriptions for altitude sickness and malaria. These had to be private prescriptions, so were also costly.

I was given Diamox for altitude sickness –, acetazolamide – a carbonic anhydrase inhibitor, causing you to excrete bicarbonate, making the blood more acidic. So as the body equates to the carbon dioxide concentration in the blood, there is a deepening of, and an increase in respiratory rate, to increase oxygen intake. This in part will counter the lower atmospheric oxygen concentration, and partly help overcome the problems caused by altitude. Only a help though, not a complete prevention.

As an anti-malarial, I was prescribed Malarone. This I would need to start taking two days before I flew, and for seven days after my return. The dilemma here was that above 1800 metres, mosquitoes do not survive. For much of the trip we would be above this, except at Addis Ababa airport, and possibly in Moshi. I had them anyway, and if I decided to take them, hoped I would not suffer from any side effects.

Vaccinations: I was up to date apparently with tetanus, and hepatitis A, so just needed hepatitis B and smallpox. This was arranged at my own health centre and done by the nurse there. Yellow fever was not done here so I would have to arrange an appointment at a surgery that did offer this facility, and I was given a list of those in the area that did. Dr Underwood then wished me luck, and said he was quite envious of me going on this expedition.

I managed to arrange an appointment in Wellington, and had to go through the procedure of registering as a temporary patient, paying £70 for the vaccination and then receiving it. I would have to admit to suffering some side effects from this vaccination. Fever, malaise for a couple of days, but it was done. Again, the requirements of Tanzania – inoculation was required if entering the country by land or from an endemic region. For us, it probably wasn't necessary as it transpired, but having had it done, there shouldn't be any complications.

So that completed the medical side of things.

I received a list of basic equipment to take from the tour operators, fairly self-explanatory, and so the next decision was how much of this I should buy, and how much I could borrow. I essentially made my decision on what I was likely to use again in the future, the rest, having friends who climbed and camped a lot (thanks Alex and Roxanne, Dave and Lisa), I would borrow from them.

There is a very good outward bound shop in Shrewsbury, Cotswold Outdoors that I went into to get what I would need to buy. One of their guys had done the climb in March 2012, and was able to give me a lot of helpful advice. Perhaps the biggest decision was that I had a very comfortable pair of walking boots, but was not sure 100% whether they were entirely waterproof, and I didn't want wet, cold feet in the sub-zero temperatures near the summit. I did therefore buy a rather expensive pair of boots, but was still undecided which pair to wear probably until about two weeks before I set off.

From the start, the idea of this trek was to try and satisfy a lifetime ambition. I was doing this for me, but while I was at a Serendipity evening in the spring, and had talked of doing the walk in the summer, it had kindled more than a little interest among other members of the club. So it was suggested to me by one, Dave Ridgeway, that if I was doing it, then perhaps I should also try and raise a bit of money for charity as well. A few days later, I was at the christening of my niece, and knowing that my ex-wife did voluntary work at Severn Hospice, I approached her as to whom I might speak to about raising money for them. As it happened, one of the hospice fundraising organisers was at the christening too, and so I was introduced to Pat Hayward. We chatted about my trip and that I was willing to try and raise money for the hospice in the process. She would e-mail me sponsorship forms and would offer any support she could. That was in place.

Being busy, I can't say I went overboard in trying to raise money, but am grateful to a couple of the ladies at Serendipity for going round people at the Tuesday night social events, getting them to sign on the dotted line, and also to all those at work, colleagues and clients, who generously put their hands in their pockets to sponsor the old codger who was going to try and climb a mountain. And some of them were very generous – a big thanks to them for their support.

At last, all was organised, I was just about ready to go.

4. PLANNING THE WALK

Along with the planning of the trip in terms of health, tickets, visas etc., etc., the other major issue was how physically I was going to prepare myself for something I have never done before, climb a mountain. Yes, over the years I had shown more than a passing interest in articles about the climb, and the occasional celebrity climb that was done for Comic Relief a couple of years previously, although that was climbed by a different, quicker route and by a group of people of different fitness levels.

I basically had two challenges. Firstly, the distance that we were going to walk, and secondly, the altitude and how to cope with the likely chance that I would at some stage succumb to it to some degree.

So, I put together a plan that I would walk as much as I could at weekends and evenings, and I also enrolled at one of the gyms in Shrewsbury to try and do some cardiovascular exercise, just to get me fitter. Shropshire is blessed with hills and many interesting walks, so just getting out wasn't going to be hard. Serendipity also did walks every Sunday so I could go on these as well. I also decided that before I went, I would go down to Exmoor, and my parents, and spend a few days there walking on the moors.

My first walk, and repeated several times over the following few weeks, was The Wrekin, a hill rising out of the Shropshire Plain to the west of Telford. Rising to a height of 407 metres, it offers a variety of different walks, up and down the stone track to the signal station near the top, straight on down the other side and then back around the bottom to the car park, and many other paths that I have since discovered over and around it. Not a long walk, but a brisk uphill slog not taking much more than twenty-five minutes to get to the top along a windy track through the forest on the lower slopes, and then onto open hillside and the exposure to the elements. It has a wonderful legend about its formation concerning a grumpy giant, but that is a diversion. It is a good, quick walk and had the advantage of being on my way home from work, so it was easy to take that slight detour to spend an hour or so walking it.

I did go on one Serendipity walk, some eight miles around paths close to where I work at Hanwood, Bayston Hill, and Nobold, but found the pace too slow for my needs, so an enjoyable social walk, but it wasn't going to give me the intensity I was looking for.

As it happened, my son then gave me for my birthday, a book – *50 Walks in Shropshire*, which gave me other ideas of where to go, even hidden away around Telford. I started with a two-hour walk beginning in Coalbrookdale, at the centre of the Industrial Revolution. The walk took me past the museums of our industrial heritage before turning away from the river, up the hill towards Telford, around the top, before descending back down into the gorge. I discovered the picturesque Lydbrook Dingle, a pretty stream flowing down the slopes towards the Severn, before heading back up above Ironbridge to a wonderful viewpoint where the Rotunda once stood, looking down the gorge and the Ironbridge of Brunel.

Back down steep wooded slopes to return past the pub – well, I deserved a drink – and back to the car.

A colleague at work told me that he thought probably the steepest hill around was Pontesford and Earl's hill, just outside Pontesbury. Again close to work, I was able to do this walk one sunny spring evening. Yes, it was a hard walk up through the pine trees, steep, and dry underfoot so it was easy to lose your footing. But once the slog through the forest was completed, on to grassy slopes to the summit and the reward, like from the top of The Wrekin, fantastic views over the whole of Shropshire and beyond to the east and north. Again, not a long walk, but certainly hard work, and then taking a slightly more sedate route back to the car park.

Another walk I did twice but starting in different places was again in the Ironbridge Gorge, walking along the banks of the Severn before crossing in Jackfield, and then turning up the hill at the Bedlam Furnaces (ruins), towards Madeley, through pergolas and steps to the Golden Ball pub, then gradually climbing higher above the river into and through woodland on the outskirts of Telford, coming out by the famous Victorian village, Blist Hill. The walk then follows the outer perimeter before meandering though woodland, past the remnants of the old canal, before turning back down the hill beside the Hay Incline back to the river and back to the car. Again a brief glimpse of our past, and along the way a total of eight pubs. Just my luck that the first time I did the walk, having parked at The Woodbridge, having arrived back there, I was greeted in the doorway by the barman, wanting to know what I wanted. Believe it or not, a pint, but as I was only the second person to walk through the door (or in my case, nearly walk through the door), he had decided he was closing. I drove up the road to The Brewery Inn, and on entering was again asked what I was doing, he was closing in ten minutes. I explained that I was doing Kilimanjaro, and for Severn Hospice, so in the end he was quite happy to offer me the sustenance I needed to wet my palate, Shropshire Gold. I did repeat this walk again but this time starting from Bedlam Furnaces, and taking a pint along the way at The Boat Inn at Coalport. A walk that can be started in several places along the route, and with plenty of places to stop for refreshment.

That in essence was my Shropshire walking, other than a few walks around Haughmond Hill, again offering different routes, and different lengths of walks. Shropshire has a lot to offer, and I didn't even touch the Shropshire Hills.

And so it was time to take myself down to the South West to try some serious walking, the idea being to walk every day for a week, and taking in one long walk to test myself that I could do it, and here I will indulge myself a little in what was a wonderful week's hiking.

5. EXMOOR, MAY 2012

Saturday, May 19th

I planned an early start, taking in a drop off at East Midlands airport on the way (Davina and a friend there on their way to Sardinia), before heading down south to go down to stay with Graham for a couple of days in Stokeinteignhead, and then onto Mum and Dad's on Exmoor until the following Saturday when I would return back to Telford.

As I left Shrewsbury in the early hours of the morning, it was dark and drizzling slightly. Little traffic on the road got us to East Midlands without much delay, and so delivering the ladies to the departure lounge to check in with their luggage, I was ready to get on MY way. Poor girls, the queues were awful and despite being there nearly two hours before their flight, they were still queuing when the flight was called, and had to be rushed through.

For me, the open and quiet road, but then the heavens opened and for the next hour I drove through torrential rain. This could become a fun holiday. As I approached Gloucestershire and more familiar country, and the sun, yes, the sun, was starting to rise, and the black clouds were dispersing – it was looking a bit better. I was making good time as well. I had arranged to meet Graham at a restaurant/cafe on the beach in Shaldon, overlooking the Teign as it enters the sea, for about eight thirty. A venture one of the barmaids from the Church Inn had just started with her boyfriend, Graham was keen to support it. And while I was driving, all the news was of the arrival of the

Olympic Torch onto our shores as it started its route around the United Kingdom, to end up in London in August. The trail would start at Land's End as I was driving, with Ben Ainslie starting it off on its long relay.

Having phoned Graham to tell him I was having a good run, I arrived safely in Shaldon on time to meet him, on what now was a glorious summer's morning with the sun reflecting off the calm sea waters. A lovely breakfast in what looked to be a nice restaurant in the making, a stroll along the beach, and then back to his house.

From here, we undertook my first walk of the week, a similar path to that we had taken back before Christmas, up the fuzzy D, a rough bridle path where once a year, people race down the hill from the top, the fastest being acclaimed the champion for the next twelve months (Graham was a past champion!). A walk that then took us over the hills towards Shaldon, following bridle and footpaths, with wonderful views over the Teign estuary, to the golf club on top of the hill the other side, and then the coastline stretching past Exmouth and away to the east. Back down into the valley and eventually back into Stokeinteignhead, and his house, perhaps I was puffing a little too much for this walk. A social trip as well, so having done five miles, we rested, enjoyed the sun, and then made the usual pilgrimage down to the Church House Inn.

The following day, May 20th, we did a similar walk, Molly accompanying us this time, but heading further towards the outskirts of Shaldon, and back above Combeteignhead. A similar distance to yesterday, so putting another five miles on the clock.

The real excitement of the day was yet to come; the Olympic Torch was coming to South Devon, and there was to be a relay over the bridge over the estuary between Shaldon and Teignmouth. The opportunity was there to see it, a once in a lifetime experience, so do it. We took ourselves down to the bridge and found a good vantage point, sitting on a high wall where we could observe it as it went past, meeting several of the other villagers we knew. It was quite a party atmosphere. Eventually a procession of police cars, a bus carrying other torch bearers (one was to be a member of a famous local band, The Muse), and then the torch bearer himself surrounded by a group of police persons in their special Olympic running kit. The design of the torch was quite spectacular, impressive, passing close by, and then it was gone. A brief look at something that would go all around the country, but I'm glad we made the effort to see it.

And so, with ten miles on the clock, and always a pleasure to stay in the village with Graham and Molly, it was time to move on up to Exmoor.

*

May 21st, and a fond farewell to them both, carrying their good luck wishes, I travelled the hour and a half journey up to Mum and Dad's on Exmoor. The weather certainly looked set fair now as I drove past Exeter, Tiverton, and followed the road up along the Exe valley. And there in front of me, the Olympic bus again, with a few unlit torches standing upright inside. Its passage today would be in North Devon and Somerset, and I had debated taking my parents up to Dunster to see it, but decided against it due to the amount of standing it may involve.

A quiet lunch and then while they enjoyed the afternoon sun, I would take myself off for another walk. I parked my car in Winsford and walked out of the village towards Withypool, up a steepish hill, before heading off across fields towards Nethercote, across Bye Hill and Bye Common. The path took me eventually down to the Exe, and I then followed the river back towards Larcombe Foot (where my uncle's ashes are scattered). I love this walk along this part of the Exe, so peaceful, in the middle of nowhere. Dippers on the river, green meadows running down to its bank, this is England. From

Larcombe Foot, I continued to follow the river back towards Winsford, through small meadows, before taking a path back up to the road I had walked up to begin with, and then following the road back down the hill to my car.

A lovely, peaceful, and relaxing walk in the afternoon sunshine, I really enjoyed it and the miles were clocking on. Back to my parents for tea and a chat, and my plans for the next couple of days.

A morning shopping trip to Dulverton on May 22nd, where in the local stores, we tracked down some Kendal Mint Cake to take with me to Africa, and then we went to lunch at the Royal Oak at Withypool, and a nice pint of Exmoor Gold. My plan today was to walk from here to Simonsbath along the Two Moors Way (a path that starts in South Devon, running across Dartmoor and Exmoor, before finishing on the North Devon Coast, today just doing part of it). I would have ridden along this way, years before, but couldn't remember it that well.

I set off along Kitridge Lane out of the village, heading west after a good lunch in the pub, and in glorious sunshine once again. A steady climb along a quiet country lane, stopping now and again, but after some time finding that I had mislaid my mobile phone. Could I have left it in the pub, in Dad's car, or dropped it? What to do. Should I retrace my steps? What were the chances of finding it? Slim. I decided I would go back and eventually came to a stile I had stopped at earlier, and there sitting on one of the upright posts, was my phone. What relief. How lucky am I!

Back up the hill again before meeting Lanacre Lane, where I left the road and headed across open moorland, disturbing a group of Exmoor ponies on the way. As I crossed the moor, one of two reasons I had wanted to do this walk today was to view Lanacre Bridge below me, a wonderful old stone bridge crossing the River Barle in the middle of nowhere. Some of these Exmoor bridges are wonderful sights. The path took me on above the Barle as it snaked its way through the valley below, before I started dropping down closer to the river, with a forestry plantation on my right. A couple of fords, and then the other reason, an old fort named Cow Castle, sitting on a loop of the river. Teaming with song birds, the noise of the river, watching the fish, to me I was in my element. I just had to stop and take all this in.

Onwards following the river, and starting to climb, I then came to the (disused) Wheal Eliza mine, an old tin mine from the nineteenth century, but still the ruins remain. The signs of forgotten times. On along the river, following the path just above it, birds and butterflies to keep me company until Simonsbath came into sight. Through beech trees the path went on until it hit the main road, and just as I stepped out onto the road (very well timed), Dad arrived in his car to meet me.

This was a really enjoyable walk.

*

May 23rd, and now the main reason I had come. Over the past four days I had walked over twenty miles. But, I wanted to know that I could walk over a long distance and over a long time period. I had come across a long walk, some thirty-six and a half miles, The Coleridge Way, a walk taken and named after the romantic poet, Samuel Coleridge, where he had walked to see his friend and fellow poet William Wordsworth in those years gone past. A walk that I had decided to do over two days, with my parent's house not far from the walk, at about the twenty-five mile point. There was the plan, to walk this distance in two days, crossing three lots of moorland: the Quantocks, the Brendons, and Exmoor itself. This would take me from Nether Stowey near Taunton, to Porlock, stopping at Luxborough. A bold plan to do by myself, a trip people often take three or four days to do.

I left my car in Luxborough (my reward for getting this far later in the day would be a pint in the Royal Oak here), and

Mum and Dad, who had business near Nether Stowey, picked me up and took me there, dropping me off just outside the cottage that Coleridge had lived in, the start of the walk. About ten thirty in the morning, I waved them off and after admiring the cottage set off following the signs, marked by a feather pen. Opposite the cottage was a pub aptly named The Ancient Mariner.

The route took me out of the village by road before joining a bridle path, and footpaths, following a stream, and then following a lane as one starts to climb towards the Quantocks. From here one picks up a path signposted "Greenway". You follow this path up the side of a field, ascending past an old quarry and entering a wood, mature beech trees with the sun shining through. Near here is the sight of Walford's Gibbet, a bloke who was hung for the murder of his wife in 1789, and hung in a cage there for a year and a day. Following the recent rains, it was quite mushy underfoot through the woods, but very peaceful, and as I continued through the woods, I eventually emerged into open heathland, skirting around the Iron Age Dowsbrough Hill Fort. From up here, magnificent views across the Quantocks, to the east, the Mendips, with the Bristol Channel and Wales in front of me. Down the hill towards the A39 and then turning towards the village of Holford, then down a lane towards Alfoxton Park, a place where Wordsworth lodged for a time. This was now fairly easy walking, and along here I came across a deer, grazing in the adjacent pastures, not willing to stay long enough to have their photo taken.

Continuing further along the path, I emerged from the woodland into open ground and as I followed the contours of the hill, crossing several combes, a sea mist was forming over the channel and threatening to come my way, bringing a chill to the air as it drifted over. This path followed the main road below me, before I turned into St. Audrie's Forest, following the logger's path before emerging by the Windmill Inn in West Quantockhead, from where I followed the road through the village, texting Margaret as to my progress. Turning uphill off the road again took me into some lovely woods, walking along their edge with the views of the Brendons to the west, and then turning downhill towards the main road, the A358, crossing this and entering the village of Bicknoller. I had aimed to be here at lunchtime, one o'clock. I was ten minutes late but making good progress, 9.6 miles done. It seemed rude not to go into the Bicknoller Inn for a well-earned pint before continuing on my way. By now it was hot, with blue sunny skies and a slight breeze, so walking was very pleasant. I had told Mum and Dad I would keep them informed of my progress, but as usual in this area, no phone reception.

Following the path out of the village and crossing a paddock, I then had to cross the a railway line, then fields and tracks and along a lane following a big stream before entering the village of Samford Brett, and picking up a path to Aller through a really old fashioned manor-type farmyard, and then striking uphill beside a very large field of broad beans. I had to assume I was still heading in the right direction as I hadn't seen the Quill for some time, but eventually emerged out of this field onto a road, finding a sign to Stogumber. Yes, I was alright, as this was mentioned on my route instructions.

Following this road a short distance I then turned off downhill again, following a hedge down into Monksilver. I had seen the signs many times, but never been there. A picturesque village, the Notley Arms pub, and then through a pretty churchyard, picking up a bridle path just past the Old Rectory, and starting to climb again up Birds Hill. Here I did find the instructions a bit vague and started to get a bit despondent, as I continued along this sodden track through woods, and not seeming to find the next path I was looking for, in fact finding signs for Raleigh's Cross. I wondered if it was easier to make my way towards there, where I knew where I was. In the end I cut across a couple of paths, down a hill onto the main road, walking towards Chigley, and by chance found a Quill, I was still on track. That's what I thought anyway, as I followed the path on towards Roadwater, following a hedge, into woods and out the other side, along a mature beech hedge to come to a crossroads of paths. But the signs said I was still three miles away from Roadwater, just the same as I was when I started along this way. And the signs were not helpful, seeming to send me back the way I had come. Decisions, decisions. Which way should I go? When it dawned on me I had been here before, I had walked round in a long circle. I guess that little detour had put another three miles on my journey, hey ho!

Another try, and I took another turn in the woods that seemed to get me back with what the instructions said. Through Pit Wood, fields, and then Erridge Wood, reaching a lane and then this leading me into Roadwater, at last. I was behind schedule now, but still no phone reception, and no time to stop at the pub. I was now following the road to Luxborough, my last stop for the day, and then turning off into Langridge Wood, climbing again and starting to feel tired. This was quite hard work before emerging into open ground at the top and then crossing fields towards farm buildings. I did manage to speak to Dad at this stage, who had been trying to ring me to see how I was, and said he knew where I was and could drive there. I was, despite being tired, now determined to reach Luxborough by foot and have a well-earned Exmoor Gold in the Royal Oak.

I think the next part in the guide says "the bridle path can be a bit muddy". All I can say is the stinging nettles along there were as tall as me, but slowly but surely the path started to descend and wind its way into Luxborough. I had achieved part 1, 23.2 miles (plus the three-mile detour). The furthest I had walked in a day, although in 2013 I did walk the London Marathon course for charity, a moon walk, but not quite the same hills in that.

The Exmoor Gold (a lovely pint of beer) went down well, then back to my parents for supper and an early night. My walk would begin tomorrow where it had ended today.

*

May 24th. Dad dropped me off in Luxborough at about nine thirty and we arranged that he and Mum would pick me up in Porlock at about two, two thirty at the latest. I had just less than fourteen miles to do but it would be harder going than yesterday, a lot more gradients and some walking over the Moor.

Again as I set off up the lane towards Newcombe Farm, the sun was shining bright and it was pleasantly warm. I was walking west towards Wheddon Cross, across fields grazed by sheep, past the trig point on Lype Hill at 423 metres, on across fields and eventually reaching Cutcombe Cross. Here, again, I found the instructions a bit vague and it was only with the help of a farmer that I managed to point myself in the right direction again to reach the A396, to follow a path taking me towards the Raleigh Manor Hotel. Shortly before the hotel I turned right, following the fence around the hotel, crossing a field that had the most glorious red beeches in and then entering Blagdon Wood.

A lovely old beech wood, I followed the path on before reaching a sign that was so vague I didn't know which way to go. I went one way, retraced my steps, tried another, but that didn't seem right either. I eventually went back onto the first route I had tried and thought if I was following the stream on my right I couldn't be far off. I was very frustrated and now way behind the clock, as this wasn't easy walking, but I did eventually emerge from the wood to find the sun had gone and an Exmoor mist was coming down.

The Coleridge Way then takes you around the eastern slopes of Dunkery Beacon, the highest point on Exmoor, following a fence on the right, through Hanny Combe towards Brockwell, and then towards Webber's Post. A pity the views were not better because of the mist. Arriving at Webber's Post you are looking at the ancient Horner Wood, and from here it was hard walking as the path starts to descend, quite steeply in places, and hard on those knees. I was behind time but now had a spring in my step as I knew where I was. A goodish stretch downhill before coming into Horner where I had stopped with my parents previously for a Devon tea, heading towards Porlock, then over the Packhorse Bridge I had admired from the car many times, and heading towards Luckbarrow. I didn't have far to go, as I reached the outskirts of Porlock, followed The Drang and Marley Row into the High Street, reaching the point where the road forks to the right to Porlock Weir, marking the end of the Coleridge Way.

I had done it, with one or two diversions, and now just had to find my parents who were getting a little worried about my non-appearance and had apparently been into the visitor centre to raise their alarms. I had received a couple of failed calls, but as usual, no reception. I bumped into Dad in the High Street after I had wandered up and down a couple of times. We went back to the visitor centre to say I was safe, signed the register of those that had done the "Way", and I raised the point about the poor signs in Blagdon Woods.

We found the car and a worried mum, and set off back home for a well-earned rest.

A walk I would thoroughly recommend taking in the Brendons, Quantock, and Exmoor – a vast range of scenery and wildlife which perhaps should be enjoyed over a longer period than my two days.

Since I did this, The Coleridge Way has now been extended to Lynmouth, taking in Watersmeet, which I think is a lovely setting, and perhaps one day I will try and do it again, with its extension, making it now fifty-one miles, and one can then go further along the South West Coast Path.

*

May 25th. Today would be a quiet day, spending some time with Mum and Dad, Mum obviously worried about the trip but trying to keep it to herself, as she knew how much I wanted this. Obviously tired, I restricted my walking today to a stroll in Kennisham Woods with them both, exercising their dog, Piper.

No more than a couple of miles, just to loosen up again, and just to enjoy their company. I didn't know when I would next see them, but it would be after my return from Africa, and possibly the autumn. In the morning I would be heading back to Telford, preparations nearly complete.

And so it was, their wedding anniversary, but I left them to enjoy it together, and back to Shropshire I came. I had walked probably nearly seventy miles over the course of the week, had succeeded in my endurance walk, which was up and down hills, though not anywhere near what I had coming. I had enjoyed wonderful weather, linked up with the Olympics, and it had been really peaceful.

Just one more climb to do.

*

June 11th. I had wanted to do one last but arduous climb before going to Africa, at least a fortnight before departing, and then leaving my fitness to be what it was. My friend Jenny had offered to help in any way, and so we decided we would do Snowdon together. Jenny an avid walker, had done it before and by different routes. I had been a couple of years previously and climbed from Llanberis, the easiest route.

Jenny had decided she would take me up the mountain along the Watkins Path, but taking a detour to climb Aran as well.

I had been working that weekend so wasn't sure what time I could leave, but would pick her up as soon as I could after my stint had finished, so we set off about eight o'clock towards Snowdonia, via Llangollen and into the more remote parts of North Wales, heading towards Llanberis before turning onto the A498 to Beddgelert. We parked the car at Bethania. The first part of the walk was on a tarmac track, gently going uphill and into woodland, before going through a gate and following a stone track up the hill, with the peak of Snowdon in front of us. After a while, there was a fork in the paths, the right fork being the Watkins Path, but we headed left towards the smaller peak of Aran. A steady uphill walk across the slope, until we reached a stone wall that we followed further up, until near the top of Aran. Crossing the wall, it was then a scramble over a very rocky path, until we reached the top at 2451 feet (sorry, old map). It had clouded over by now, and was quite chilly as we viewed Snowdon to our north, and looking towards the coast to our west.

A light sustenance, and then we retraced our steps down a little way before taking a path towards Snowdon. We went down quite a long way, and then came across a barbed wire fence that we would have to cross and then straddle a stream. For the only time on this walk, I was of some use to Jenny, knowing how to deal with these obstacles, and having overcome them, we skirted around a small lake, quite boggy underfoot, and then started to climb, taking the route up the south ridge of Snowdon. Bare earth, rock, and some crags that we had to haul ourselves up, this I did find hard work. Jenny, climbing as nimble as a mountain goat, assured me there would be nothing as bad as this on Kilimanjaro. We went further and further up, unrelenting hard work, seeing the occasional groups of people doing the same route. By now the cloud had come down and visibility wasn't that good. We took the occasional break for a drink, and did reach one point where I was beginning to feel a little light headed and said I would have to stop and get some energy into me, probably a result of my rushed start to the day and being low in calories.

The south ridge gets rockier, and rockier, but eventually, out of the mist was the summit, with its fancy viewing house and cafe. A stop for a sandwich here, although we couldn't really enjoy the views because it was so cloudy now, and we were up in them. And then we started down.

We followed the south ridge down a short way before

turning east, and started to zigzag down a path which became less distinct the further we went on, to the point I wondered if we were actually on a path. It also became more loose scree underfoot, and I had to take this part very steadily, especially with the strain it was putting on my ankles. I certainly didn't enjoy this part of the walk, and was quite relieved when we returned to a more distinct path. We did come across one small group of people who were in distress, having left the path and headed straight up the scree, losing their confidence. From above, we had to guide them step by step towards us, telling them where to place their hands, which way to go. The women seemed really scared, but Jenny got them to safer ground, and then we continued on our way, circling around under the crags, Bwlch Ciliau, to a point where you have fantastic views of the other mountains in this region, Llyn Llydaw below on the other side of the ridge.

Jenny told me how she had once done some challenge where you do all these mountains, twenty something, I think she said, in a limited time, and she succeeded despite spraining her ankle early on. Under the shelter of the ridge, we stopped to eat our lunch, and then continued steadily down, zigzagging down the slope until we reached a disused mine site. By now, with the summit being left behind us, the weather was improving again, and it was pleasant walking as we continued down on a better track. We passed Gladstone Rock, a commemorative rock to celebrate the then Prime Minister, Gladstone, addressing the locals in 1892.

A little further down as we start to follow a river, Afon Cwym Llan, we came across the most magnificent waterfall, or series of waterfalls, which for me made this trip worthwhile. Truly spectacular and Jenny couldn't understand why I found this better than Snowdon. I love fast-flowing water. After watching the water flow down for a while, we continued back down the path, back to the gate we had started at and returned down the road to the car.

About five hours altogether, and we had put in some hard

yards especially on the south ridge. But we had done it – a thoroughly enjoyable day, memorable for the waterfall, and for that climb to the summit.

My training was over.

Back into the car, we set off back to Telford, listening to England play France at football, and we nearly won! I was going to have a quiet evening. Jenny, she was to go off dancing. Where does she find the energy!

All that was left for me to do now was to decide what to take, and go.

The Olympic Torch in Shaldon, Devon.

Across Exmoor, Lannacre bridge.

Cow Castle and the River Barle, Exmoor.

Follow the quill, the Coleridge Way.

Across the Quantocks on the Coleridge Way.

And on towards the Brendons.

Waterfalls, the Watkins Path, Snowdon.

Up Snowdon, and the clouds came down.

6. TIME TO GO
JUNE 23-27TH

So after all the planning, the preparation, the walks, it was now time to go. The biggest thing now in my mind with just a few days to go before the flight was that it was definitely going to happen and happen very soon. I had decided that I was going to take it easy the weekend before I went, so it was about sorting in my mind what I needed to take, making sure I had it, and then adding it to my pile on the spare bed. Tuesday and Wednesday morning would be decision day as to what was going, and what I would leave behind. Try and relax with all the chaos going on around me was the order of the day.

Little piles were developing: protective clothing, warm "inner" wear, shoes and boots, travel clothing, casual clothing for the hotel, snacks and medicines, cameras and spare batteries, torch, glasses, etc. And a collection of rucksacks, holdalls, sleeping bag, light mattress, warm liner to sleep in, books, notepad and pens. On Saturday I went into Cotswolds in town to get extra shoelaces, another water bottle and some light inner socks to wear inside my walking socks for warmth on the final ascent. I can't remember who recommended these but it was better to have them just in case temperatures were very low.

After a lifetime of wanting to do this, I was just killing time now before the flight on Wednesday, going through my mind all I might want, to be able to minimise it to what I was allowed to travel with in my luggage allowance. Making sure I had the essentials, and then I could pad it all out with snacky things – Kendal Mint Cake, ginger biscuits (which I had been told were good for altitude) if I had any spare weight to go with. And then, to arrange it to maximise cargo luggage. Walking boots would be heavy, so I had to squeeze them in hand luggage, little things like that.

I had decided on a quiet weekend before, sorting last things out, but mainly just relaxing, having a short walk on Haughmond Hill, but nothing strenuous, to just unwind. Monday and Tuesday morning I was due to work, finishing at lunchtime from when I would have twenty-four hours to myself, planning to leave at one o'clock Wednesday lunchtime. If a little quiet over this time, it was probably just finalising in my mind what I was about to do and organising myself for it. Very much a list person, I had done most of my preparations and it was now just a matter of crossing them off as I went along, but not rushing or stressing myself over it.

So a steady day at work on Monday, which was good to keep my mind off things, and also Tuesday morning, a bit quieter so dragged a little. Lunchtime came and the office was quiet so my leaving went virtually unnoticed, with no-one wishing me well – but then I didn't want a fuss over it. Though the money for charity was partly raised from farmers and members of staff, it was ultimately a personal quest so the quieter the better as far as I was concerned. Go, come back in just over two weeks, and hopefully just walk in and say I did it.

So home, and to my packing. A stop at the bank on the way home to pick up my pre-ordered Tanzanian shillings – the staff were interested in my trip. The last item was now collected to travel. Everything was either going in a large holdall which would be easy to carry from camp to camp, or in my rucksack that I would carry myself. We had been given a list of essential and recommended equipment to take, so they were the priorities in my piles on the floor. Warm clothing, a few layers including gloves, water bottles and food, sleeping bag, liners, basically night-time stuff to try and keep warm with a little bit of comfort, basic clothing, wash stuff, camera, phone, batteries, note book, and then what one may term luxury items which if there was room could go, if not then no worries.

So, I think everything was now on the lounge floor in these piles, plus the important travel documents, money, yellow fever certificate, etc., which would travel on my personage. Items like sleeping bags were light and already rolled up tightly so they went in the bottom of the holdall, and then I packed around these. Slowly the piles disappeared, and the floor started to clear. I didn't want to do it all that evening, so called time on it with all the major items in, checking on weight, but by then I probably knew what I wouldn't be taking. I had also decided that some of the clothing I was taking, I would leave for the Tanzanian porters' collection which I had been told about in the brochures, making coming back far easier.

The evening would be spent with a light supper, water the garden, and then having a quiet drink by the river in the Ironbridge gorge at The Boat Inn. Just a couple of pints, a walk back over the bridge to the car, and back home for an early night and what I hoped would be a good night's sleep. Being a poor sleeper, I suspected this could be the last decent night's sleep until my quest had either failed or succeeded. I was relaxed, so didn't take to bed all my worries of the trip, packing, success or failure. Probably if I did have a wish it was that I could just get up and go, rather than twiddling my fingers until lunchtime and my planned time of departure.

Sleep came easily, dawn probably a bit too quickly, but the day had finally arrived, my expedition was really about to start. There was no need to rush to get up, so I lay in bed and organised my mind, got up, had breakfast, then it was just to finish packing and check the garden over, which Davina was going to come over and keep watered as and when. Like most years, my "huge" raspberry crop was ready just as I was about to go away. Never mind, hopefully they would be enjoyed by other mouths. Back to packing: take a few things out, reorganise the holdall, last things into the rucksack, and I still have time to kill. Relax. I put the clothes I wasn't taking away, the luggage into the car, I might just as well go. It's just before two o'clock – the adventure begins.

I suppose if I did have a worry at this stage, it was probably Heathrow and driving in the outskirts of London when I didn't really know where I was going, especially if I was delayed I would be in rush hour traffic. I had sort of planned in my head where I needed to be to find my car parking, but still had to organise myself in London traffic, something I have never really enjoyed. Now I will have to do it.

A fairly easy route using the link road around Birmingham, just to avoid traffic hold-ups. M40 down, then cut across to the M4 by Windsor, off at the Heathrow turn off, Junction 3, then the difficult bit – finding the car park. No problems, a quick stop at Warwick Services for a quick snack then onwards to London. One would have to say, all day and now on the journey, it certainly wasn't what you would call a pleasant summer's day! Overcast and not that warm. I was unsure of what weather would greet me at the other end of my flight, still nearly twenty-four hours away, but hoped the weather would be better than this. Anyway, all thoughts as I made my way closer to London.

I had heard that there would be some congestion going into London, due to road works, in preparation for the 2012 London Olympics fast approaching. Luckily for me, I found these started at the junction I took to leave the M4. But, the roads were still busy as I headed south and then back on myself west towards my parking at Heathrow. As I had said, I had made a rough map in my mind and came to a very busy traffic-lighted roundabout where I knew I had to take the old A4, the Bath Road, and counting the junctions off, took what I thought was the right exit. A busy road, dual carriageway, but from instructions it didn't sound as if finding the car park should be that difficult. I travelled along this road the distance stated, expecting to find the park on my left hand side... No joy as I went through a junction with adjoining traffic, and on further. No sign of it, so all I could do was find a place to turn around, retrace my tracks, and hopefully see the car park in passing so I could easily find it after turning back up the original side. Again, nothing, and I was beginning to get a bit fraught, so finding myself somewhere to again retrace my tracks, I again headed west, tried a side road at the said distance given in my travel instructions, nothing again, and was now some thirty minutes behind where I wanted to be.

What to do? I decided to go back up to the roundabout and try again. Luckily as I approached it, I noticed that the next exit was the Bath Road, so though committed to another lane, at least I knew where I was supposed to be going. So right around and off this time at the correct exit, and it wasn't long before I had at last found my destination.

Parking here was very easy, and certainly an airport car park I would use again. Easy check and instructions, and the bus pickup was only yards away. So, a final check through my documents – yes I had everything. Sort out duplicates that could stay in the car, lock up and take my luggage to the pickup point after handing in my keys. I didn't have to wait long for a bus, not many people on it, and so it wasn't many minutes before I had arrived at Heathrow Airport proper, and after a couple of drop offs, at last had arrived at my destination, which was Terminal 3.

James, at work, had texted me to see if I could send him a picture of me departing, to put on the work website for a bit of publicity and awareness, and hopefully a bit more sponsorship. As usual, when you want to find someone, there was no-one about, but luckily another bus pulled in and a young lady got off it. I approached her and said what I was about to do and she was only too willing to help, using the camera on my phone. The picture I hoped I could then get around my technological barriers to forward on to James. A lovely lady, we chatted about my lifetime ambition and found she also was a walker, soon to have a go at the Three Peaks challenge. We wished each other luck and went our separate ways.

Entering the terminal, I found my check in area very easily, and so was able to offload my holdall very quickly, go through passport control and into the departure lounge very swiftly. All done by 1815 hours so back on track with my schedule, but still a fair while before the flight was due to take off at 2100 hours. At least I was there and was not rushing. I had planned just to be there in plenty of time to allow for delays through the airport, and to have time for a decent meal, a drink, a last few texts or phone calls, before boarding. I had achieved this.

I would have to admit that other than dropping off and picking up, I had never actually been inside Heathrow before, and although perhaps Terminal 3 is the quietest, or perhaps least busy of the three, I was surprised how busy it was. People everywhere, and from what I could see, quite a few who looked as if they were heading for Kilimanjaro. Who would be going with me? Some looked large parties of teenagers or perhaps university students, others in organised groups.

Just somewhere to sit for a while would be good, I had been dragging this rucksack around long enough. It was no turning back now, so just me time, to unwind from work, packing, the drive down, and the fiasco of finding the car park. But, part of the adventure was to do all this by myself, and here I was very much alone amongst all these people at Heathrow. I feel good, and am unwinding. Though noisy, and with my hearing, not that easy, time to make a couple of phone calls while I have a chance. A last phone call to Mum and Dad to say I was at the airport. Mum worried about the trip and the risks, but she has to worry about something. But knowing I had wanted to do this for so long, there was still much encouragement and I would let her know when I had achieved my goal which she was sure I would. Dad offered his full support and interest in my itinerary over the next few days, whether I had met my party yet, a general chat, and that was that.

I knew they were worried, but also knew they respected my ambitions and determination in trying to achieve my goals, and after depression, how important it was for me to try, even if I didn't succeed. "Goodbye and I will speak to you soon," were my departing words. Next, Davina. Yes, I was at the airport safely and waiting to board. I checked on who she was to contact on my say so, when I knew my destiny, success or failure, but at least letting everyone know I was safe. I think people close to me were more worried than I was, but if nothing else, that showed I had cleared my mind of all that had gone on the previous few years, and I was happy with myself (even if there was a small amount of doubt in my mind, but I'm off).

A meal would be nice and a final drink before we fly. I didn't know when would be the next time I would get a decent pint before I flew back, so I find one of the bar/restaurants there and order (not really me, but it's British), fish and chips and a pint of London Pride, and then (more difficult), find somewhere to sit and eat and drink my last meal. The food was okay, the pint was very enjoyable, and while finishing this off, one last phone call. Jenny had been fantastic in helping my preparations, encouragement, and advice from her of her climb of the same mountain, and just useful tips. The trek up Snowdon was a great help in my preparation for the climb, and great fun as well. Not always easy to get on the phone, she did actually answer, so it was nice to have a chat about the climb rather than people worrying about me. A chat for ten minutes or so, and yes, I had got the ginger biscuits to help with altitude sickness and a fond farewell and thanks for her help.

A few minutes to collect myself, finish the Pride, and time to move on towards the departure gate. Time was getting nearer to departure. It's 1945 hours, and a call to go.

I suppose it shows the vastness of the airport that, rucksack in tow, I then had a considerable walk and ride on escalators to the departure lounge for our flight. Obviously by now, most people I saw were either carrying a rucksack and boots like me, or were dressed in what I suppose I would term traditional African dress, on their way back home, business or pleasure, holiday, see relatives... In my absence of company, people watching and guessing their reasons for the flight occupied my mind for want of anything else to do. Amongst these travellers would be somewhere, my companions for the next few days, but which ones was anyone's guess, at this stage I didn't even know how many that would be. But, it was obvious some were in organised groups which narrowed the field down.

The lounge was large and I was able to find a seat without others being on top of me. There wasn't a lot to do now but wait for our call to our gate. I had taken one book to read, and a couple of *National Geographical* magazines, and a couple of tour guides given to me, but trying to read while waiting proved to be fruitless as my head kept coming up to people watch. Time would soon pass, and the call came to go to our gate. Not the mad scramble you get on your normal tourist flights. We were travelling with Ethiopian Airlines to Addis Ababa, and from there changing flights to get to Tanzania.

Progress was quite swift, other than (I presume) Ethiopians who (I presume) were travelling First Class, kept strolling to the head of the queue and getting precedence over us mere mortals. Some had enormous amounts of hand luggage with them which seemed to stall the process.

Only to mention now that as people queued behind me, one or two stood out. I don't know why particularly, perhaps one or two who looked very young to be doing this trip, and I suppose the two that really stood out were two men, obviously travelling together, who seemed to have a great bond between them, as if in a relationship. Why I thought that I'm not sure, but it did stick in my mind, and good luck to them on their journey. Perhaps it also made me think how much I was on my own now, but that was my choosing.

Anyway, I did eventually reach the gate, everything checked okay. The last long walk to the boarding gate, and onto Flight ET701, London Heathrow to Addis Ababa, departure time 2100 hours.

I'm on the plane and there is no going back...

7. TAKE OFF

ON MY WAY: JUNE 27TH

On time, we are all boarded and it's time to go, Africa awaits me. Take off at 2100 with an arrival time of 0650 in Addis, nearly seven hours (a two-hour time difference) of flying, which I have found on past experiences is a little over my comfort time for being cooped up in a plane seat. I usually try to test my powers of geography by trying to identify landmarks through the plane window as we fly over them, but it will be dark in an hour or so. England, the Channel, and some of France is all I will see, and perhaps a sunset, though it is still overcast. We will be above the clouds so fingers crossed. I have managed to get a window seat, so at least can enjoy the "views" and not be disturbed by other people getting in and out of their seats.

For all this, the flight to Ethiopia is the one part of the trip I can remember very little about, a large gap in my mind other than being served a couple of meals. I suppose, like everyone else, that this is night and the time for sleeping, something I have never found that easy in flight due to the contortions I have to put my body through to gain some degree of comfort. How well I slept I'm not sure but I at least must have dozed a lot over the course of the night. It did seem that every time I reached something resembling sleep another meal appeared. That is not a complaint, the cabin crew were very pleasant, helpful, and one would have to comment on the stunning beauty of the female members of the crew – Ethiopian ladies, with their dark glowing complexions and very fine cheekbones. Their dress was very smart as well. Genuine beauties, these ladies.

The food was okay, hot and cleared up quickly; back to dozing. The flight passed uneventfully, long hours drifting by as we travelled over Europe, crossing the Mediterranean and then reaching Africa over the Egyptian coast, memories of the previous year when I spent a very enjoyable few days doing a Nile cruise and seeing some unbelievable and unforgettable sights. This trip included another of my top bucket list items – hot air ballooning over the Nile at sunrise. On that trip I was warmed by the welcome of the Egyptians given to us, and hospitality given throughout the trip, though the hassle from traders, etc. in trying to sell you something you didn't want and the constant asking for tips did get more than a bit tedious. I suppose everyone has to try to make a living somehow, but I was left with the overriding feeling that those who helped us most, probably got tipped least, as one loses sight of the different values of currency. As night progressed towards dawn, we had flown over arid landscapes now just about visible, nearing our intermediate destination of Addis. In better light I could have seen us cross the Mediterranean, cross over the Egyptian coast, follow the Nile for a while, before crossing over the border to the vast landlocked Sudan. But not this time; Africa from the sky would have been fascinating. I'm sure a rarity for this region but the weather had deteriorated into a light drizzle – it could have been in England still. As more people stirred on the plane, getting themselves ready for landing and the next stage, the capital of this country started to emerge through the dim light; rows and rows of street lights stretching into the distance, but on the outskirts of the town there was more basic living accommodation – huts, yards strewn with rubbish. Perhaps the reality of the visions of poorer parts of Africa that we have.

Bole International Airport is on the east side of the town, which stretches away to the west. To the east, arid land going into distant hills. We are here, so we fasten seat belts and we wait as a smooth landing takes place, on time so it's just before seven in the morning, and once we disembark, we have some time to kill before our connection to Tanzania takes off.

This is perhaps where some of naivety in travelling showed; we are changing planes although still travelling with Ethiopian Airlines, so what happens to our luggage? Do we have to collect it and check it in again or will it just automatically be taken from one plane to the other? Not all those travelling on the plane will be heading to Kilimanjaro, some will have finished their journey here. Best find someone friendly to ask when I have the chance.

We disembark from the plane, a short walk across the tarmac to a metal gate which we all trudge through, follow my leader, and we follow each other along an array of corridors and staircases, eventually coming to a wider corridor leading to what I suppose one would describe as a departure lounge. I get the chance to walk beside what look like a seasoned pair of adventurists, an older gentleman with a bush hat on, and walking boots tied around his neck, one hanging each side. His girlfriend I assume, was a pleasant-looking younger lady, but again looking ready to set off on an expedition. I take the opportunity to ask them what happens about luggage and am told from their experiences that the luggage is automatically transferred from one plane to the other. No worries then, I can just find a space to rest and pass the three and a half hours we have before we take off again.

Well!! This can only be described as the grottiest lounge I have ever been into at an airport. Seating, was minimal, though if you are lucky enough to get a seat, they do stretch out into beds. Ventilation was also minimal, a couple of fans coming down from the ceiling. Windows, I wish! Toilets at the far end, basic but adequate and did at least have a window open with views over the town. Well I'm not sure if the window actually shut. If I had some idea of what a Moroccan bazaar would look like then this was it. I can only say it was still early in the day and not too hot yet, because I can imagine in the heat of the day this could be stifling, a real sauna.

Some people managed to get the loungers and it was back to sleep for them, some did risk the food at the cafe to one side of the "lounge" but on a couple of strolls by, there was nothing that I really fancied eating, again it all looked a bit Arabic. It all became a bit like musical chairs. If someone got up from their seat, it would soon be taken by someone hovering and there was no return for the departed. I did get the chance to sit down eventually, but metal-bottomed seats are not that comfortable so in these inhospitable surroundings, time to try and read, knowing that if I want to go to the loo, that will be the end of my seated time.

Time really does drag now, it's uncomfortable and the temperature is starting to rise. On the other side of the security guards there are what look like more comfortable lounges, but although people keep asking if we can go through, it doesn't look as if this will become available before our flight is called.

Time drags, it really does.

And then at last, some movement. One or two people try security and are allowed through and wander up the corridor out of sight. It's worth a try so I get my tickets and passport out and am let through, passing a couple of lounges before reaching the one designated to our flight. There are a few people in there, but with seating available in the plenty, yes I'll go for that for a bit. One starts to recognise people seen on the previous flight, different parties, young and old. One sticks in the mind, a group of Americans in deep religious discussion, what I would call fanatical and over the top, but it is not for me to judge them on their views, and it was all a little intense for me. I couldn't really see some of these people climbing a mountain, perhaps they weren't going to!

Eventually, watching what was happening outside, a plane did land and people disembarked near our lounge, so I assumed that this would be Flight ET815, Addis Ababa to

Kilimanjaro Airport, Tanzania – the last part of our journey. Due to take off at 1020 hours, there was a slight delay but after what seemed an eternity at this airport, we were finally allowed to board. A shuffle down stairs, across a small bit of tarmac and up the steps, again to be greeted by pleasant and attractive Ethiopian air stewardesses. Again, I had been designated a window seat on the starboard side of the plane.

So, a smooth take off and we carry on travelling south across this great continent, a flight that should take just over two and a half hours, traversing Ethiopia and Kenya before landing at Kilimanjaro Airport just over the border in Tanzania. The weather has improved and although cloudy, the sun is shining. This plane is slightly smaller than our inward flight to Addis, a Boeing 737, and one would assume most of the people on the flight have one purpose, to climb the mountain by whichever route they had chosen.

The flight would take us over the arid uplands of southern Ethiopia. Fascinating to see the contrasts in scenery and landscape as we flew south, not quite desert but certainly very dry and desolate, I cannot recall see seeing any signs of habitation as we flew over, just rolling hills, dry and with occasional rocky outcrops. Obviously very different from my experiences on my Nile cruise, with rich vegetation surrounding the banks of the river either side before disappearing into sand and desert as especially to the west, the Sahara stretched into infinity. I believe there are trekking holidays in this part of the country, and that may be something to consider and explore at a later date, but I suppose the other consideration here is the political uncertainty and troubles in Somalia and Eritrea close by.

It is interesting the more one reads about this fascinating continent which is not well endowed with mountains, even though it stands relatively higher than other continents. The greater part of Africa's land surface is between 1600 and 3200 feet above sea level, but less than 1.35 percent is above 6500 feet. Many of Africa's mountains are products of volcanic activity and so in relation to others, are mere youngsters. So as we crossed Ethiopia, I have since learned that although the country only represents barely four percent of the continent's landmass, it has fifty percent of the land above 6500 feet, and just under eighty percent of the land above 9800 feet. Interesting landscapes that we flew over in northern Ethiopia as we flew into Addis at sunrise, and that were more visible from the plane as we continued our journey onwards before crossing the border into Kenya. How much this continent has to offer as one explores it more and more.

As we crossed into Kenya, this is the Africa that had fascinated me as a teenager as we started to travel down the Great Rift Valley. That amazing geographical feature of East Africa. If my recollection of it is not what it was those forty-odd years ago, its formation and topography, then the interest still existed like it always had.

Obviously from my seat on one side of the plane, my view was westwards only with Great Plains of flattish lands extending towards hills and mountains on the western edge of the Rift.

Looking greener than the scenery of Southern Ethiopia we had passed over, there was vegetation but again not that lush.

And perhaps here is a time to briefly reflect on what in my view is one of the great geographical features of the world. The East African landscape is in the most part, a vast and almost featureless plain. The plain is thrown into relief by the Rift Valley System and its volcanoes, which are in turn part of a greater single system that runs from Syria in the north down to the eastern coast of Africa just below the Zambezi River, some 3000 miles in distance. This is all as a result of the cataclysmic movements of the earth's crust some one million years ago. Over the past two million years, the African plate, Arabian plate and the Somalian plate began to move towards each other, rupturing and slumping the landscape as it did so. As the plates shifted, the Rift Valley was formed, stretching the vast distance it does. Deep fractures in the earth's crust allowed magma to surge along weak lines, and erupt from beneath the surface of the disturbed plains. Volcanoes were formed along a stretch of 100km, mentioned below. Activity that still goes on, as the plates continue to move.

The floor of this great valley varies from thirty to eighty miles wide, as can be seen from my view out of the plane window, and is characterised by a number of lakes. The Western rift stretches from Lake Tanganyika (the second deepest lake in the world) down to Lake Albert, and is characterised by a more mountainous ridge to the west. The Eastern rift, the one I can see as we fly, lies east of Lake Victoria, and cuts Kenya in two. Here most of the lakes are shallow, closed lakes in terms of drainage, and noted for the soda lakes such as Magadi. From here, the outstanding features are volcanoes rising sharply from the surrounding plains, high craggy mountains, some with snow and ice on their peaks, Kilimanjaro being the highest, and as previously stated, the highest free-standing mountain in the world as it is not part of a range. Ice and snow, yet so close to the Equator. Mount Kenya is another of these volcanoes, but has been inactive for a long time. It is only seventy-odd years however, since there was volcanic activity in Northern Tanzania. Of course there is the vast caldera of Ngorongoro, a huge crater formed from a volcano falling in on itself producing a vast and deep bowl, now so rich in wildlife. This is a place I would like to visit at a later date.

I digress, but have to mention some of the geography that has charmed me here after all those years of wanting. On with the journey.

And so as we continued southwards along the Rift Valley towards Tanzania and Kilimanjaro, the next event of note for me, a first, announced through the plane by the pilot was that we were crossing the Equator, the "mid-girth" of the world. Nothing special in terms of occasions but for me now, I had entered the southern hemisphere for the first time in my life, and I hope not the last.

And as we continued, more blue skies and large white clouds, while below could be seen more and more signs of habitation. I don't know what they are called, round huts, wooden rising to a central high point. From the height we were looking, well-constructed and solid, surrounded by a circular enclosure, with a fence and a further enclosure around all this with what looked like a bush or scrub barrier. Small areas of cultivation, and from our height I guess probably a few goats in the enclosure. These dotted around on the valley floor. This below is the Africa I had first got my interest from, and it was fantastic to see it in the flesh after all these years.

Not far to go now, as the flat plains wandered into the horizon and the uplands of the Rift, and so we cross the border over into Tanzania and the pilot announces that if we look out of our windows, to the left, yes, those on the other side of the plane have their first views of Kilimanjaro, and on the right (my side), there are views of another mountain, Meru, a neighbour of my goal, not so high but just the same, a volcano. When Jenny did her trip she and her colleagues used Meru as a warm up to acclimatise to the altitude, before tackling Kili. An impressive mountain, well, the tallest I have ever seen as I have still to get a view of Kili.

Kilimanjaro is only just over the border in Tanzania and so soon after the announcement of the view outside, it is time to fasten seat belts before we start our descent into Kilimanjaro Airport. Down, down, a smooth descent and we reach terra firma. We taxi off the runway and come to a halt on the tarmac, and await the go ahead to disembark from the plane. It is warm, very pleasant with a slight breeze as we get to the bottom of the steps and make our way to the arrivals lounge, still wondering who my walking partners will be – I will soon find out.

So, the usual clamour when the signs say stay in your seats, with all standing and retrieving their hand luggage, and waiting for the word that we can leave the plane. It comes, and in an orderly fashion we depart our transport from fore and aft. No buses, so we have a walk in the sun across the tarmac to the arrivals lounge, time to enjoy and take in my first steps in Tanzania. The airport looks very modern, obviously renovated or built to cater for the attraction and income the Kilimanjaro challenge brings for the country. Looking back towards the plane and beyond, the plains of the Rift Valley stretch into the distance, in front of me, the others, heading towards the terminal, a modern frontage but little else of note around. A few trees but that is all. But as I have said, I am very pleasantly surprised with my first impressions of this country I have thought about for so many years. How much it beats my expectations so far.

We cross the tarmac and reach the terminal through large glass doors, and meet the first inspection point. A guy in a white coat checking yellow fever vaccination certificates, and a form we had had to fill in while still on the plane about our travel plans and destinations. Fairly straight forward, so on into the arrivals lounge for passport control, and visa inspection. All seems so relaxed here, so much room, no-one fighting for space to get ahead of everyone else. I just stroll from one desk to the next, and then onto baggage collection – easy. We all do have to wait here for a short while, as the baggage too has to be unloaded and make its way across the tarmac and then put on the conveyors for us to pick our own bags. But, unlike a lot of airports, this doesn't seem to take very long and I am soon reunited with my holdall, last seen at Heathrow, but thankfully safe and sound back in my presence.

So now to find my way, to seek out my tour operator, and see who was going to be my travelling companions. I know we are only a small party, five people in total, which may be good if we all get on, not if we don't. Time to find out. I leave the back of the building, turn left and immediately bump into my operators, showing a sign for Explore and the

Lesomotho route. Two native Tanzanians, one short, with short hair, the other, darker, taller and with long plaited hair. I introduced myself, and them to me, Chunga (the shorter of the two) and William. Chunga announced himself as the tour leader, and William the walk leader. William wanted to be known as King Willi of Kili. Both were very effervescent chaps, and very welcoming. I was first, and as we stood there introducing ourselves to each other, we awaited the other four. Next, after a few minutes came Claire and Chris. It was the couple I had asked at Addis about the transfer of luggage from one plane to the next connection. We all introduced ourselves to each other. Little did I know so close to leaving England, that the trip was almost cancelled as there were only three of us going, but Claire and Chris had booked their trip only a few days previously, and with their booking the powers that be had decided that a party of five would be sufficient to go ahead. Destiny, who knows, but despite all my plans, reservations, and self-doubts, it was almost taken out of my control by insufficient interest.

Last but not least, after a while, came the last two, and yes it had to be those two guys I had seen in the queue back at Heathrow. Jeff and Neil joined us and again all the introductions, King Willi announcing himself again, but all seemed in good humour and it looked like we would be a good party.

We collect our luggage together, and it's now as if there is no-one else about who is doing the climb, as we are led to our transport to take us away from the airport. Even with only five of us, not all will go in the back of the Land Rover, so some go between the seats. I'm near the back. We head off on what are very good roads, out of the airport, through a control check manned by army personnel and off towards Moshi. A long, straight road leads us through agricultural land, maize plantations (though not looking very healthy) and the occasional goat herd on what looks very barren "pasture". A drive for a few miles, then a T-junction onto a busy main road towards Moshi. I don't know where everyone else was on the plane, but as we turned, there in front of me was my first view of what I had come to climb. Standing out in the sky was the snow-covered summit of Kilimanjaro, surrounded by clear blue sky, and a mystical grey-blue of the lower slopes making it look as if the snowy mountain was suspended in the sky. I had to be in awe of this sight, what I had dreamed of all those years, and there at last it was, rising up into the sky in front of me. But it also looked a distance away and very high. My quest, tomorrow we would be starting in the foothills our ascent of this treasure, the Roof of Africa.

The road took us past more fields of sick-looking maize, habitations lining the sides of the roads, along with more goats, and women selling their produce, mainly tomatoes. I suppose this is our first sight of the poverty that occurs in these nations. But in passing, there also seems to be a warmth exuded by the locals of this region. The road is very busy, with many trucks, new and battered, travelling in opposite directions, some buses and much activity by the roadside.

And then, the landscape changes; the fields, the maize looks lusher, healthier and more productive. It transpires these are now state-run and managed farms, so there is irrigation and everything is done on a larger scale. We cross one or two sizable streams with a reasonable flow of water descending down them. Then we turn left down a track through these maize fields, again straight for a couple of miles, and then a left turn down a very rough track. Hedged either side, where are we going. We pass a couple of buildings and then reach a compound with large gates, and an armed guard standing outside them. The gates are swung open, we proceed a few yards past a few thatched "huts", and draw up outside a plush reception area, the front of our hotel. This does look good.

So this is base camp, as it were, and we are soon ready to go. I hadn't expected anything quite like this hotel, but who is complaining?

Terminal 3, Heathrow. Departure imminent.

This way to the summit.

Relaxing at Weru Weru Hotel.

8. THE EXPEDITION BEGINS

And so the long journey south has ended and we now have arrived at the starting point of our adventure. I wasn't expecting this, but then I don't suppose I really knew what I was expecting, probably a basic hotel in town, as a base for us to start and finish from.

But this place is amazing, what a shame our time here will be so brief. Our arrival as just mentioned was through secure gates and to the reception area of the hotel. We unloaded our luggage and made our way into the reception, a spacious area with comfortable settees, and a large reception desk. Chunga took us over to this and introduced us, our party, so we were able to check in. We had to surrender our passports to the desk, but what's new with that? Chunga says he has a few things to sort out but will return to the hotel at five to give us a briefing into what we will be doing tomorrow, and an outline of the climb. We wave he and King William goodbye, to see them later.

When we had all done this we were led to our rooms. Out of the back of reception, restaurant to our right, large outdoor bar area but covered, and then onto a path, which led to six "huts". The rooms were each one named after one of the climb routes up Kili. Jeff and Neil, Chris and Claire were sharing, me, I was spoilt in having a room to myself. The others were shown their rooms. In their hut, Jeff and Neil were above the other two, and I was led further round appropriately into the Lesotho hut. My porter led me up the stairs at the side, opened the door and there was my suite. He quickly showed me round, then left after receiving his tip for me to explore this luxury myself. A large bedroom with relaxation area, chairs, settee, all the usual stuff but laid out in an African style. Off this led a large storage area, wardrobes, shelves etc., this then leading into a large bathroom. Back in the bedroom, and opening patio doors onto a balcony, overlooking the centre of the enclosure (as they all did), with the swimming pool in the centre of the lawn. This looks wonderful, so I take a few moments just to take in the views, the room.

Best course of action looks to be to unpack quickly so that I can have some relaxation by the pool, again something I hadn't expected, but it's there so let's take advantage of it. A lot of this will need to go with me when we set off tomorrow, some I will carry and some can go in my holdall, so I decide as I have so much space that I will just put everything in piles, such as sleeping stuff, warm clothing, water bottles, etc., etc., and deal with it more fully later. So I quickly do that as best I can, probably no more than fifteen or twenty minutes because that pool area does look very tempting. It has been a long time in these clothes, since I left home well over twenty-four hours ago, but a shirt, a book, and my swimming trunks and towel will do fine, all I need to take down with me. So I descend the stairs from the upper storey of my hut, walk round the front of it and to the pool. The others having been given the upstairs and lower floor of the closest hut to the pool, Jeff and Neil are already there when I get there, Chris and Claire presumably still doing some sorting.

The sun is shining, with a few white clouds in the sky, but it is warm, pleasantly warm. I find a table under a tree to deposit my things, pull up a chair in the sun and enjoy. Neil and Jeff are swimming in the pool, an interesting design, looking very rustic with edges of roughened stone, steps leading down from one end in a semi-circle, going down to a deep end with a square end. The water doesn't look that clear, but it is apparently comfortably warm. The place seems virtually deserted apart from us and a multitude of staff hovering around the bar area, with only us to attend. Chris and Claire appear as well, with books. We introduce each other properly, and chat about ourselves generally, our jobs, what we have come for and our experience at climbing. It turns out Chris is the chief rugby correspondent of *The Independent*, just back from England's tour of South Africa (that should make it an interesting trip for me), Claire his girlfriend a solicitor, younger than him. They come from just outside Bristol, so we have quite a lot in common as it turns out. A waiter comes over, and kindly, Claire buys me a beer, the local brew, Kilimanjaro beer. They have a pot of tea, Jeff and Neil already have a beer each. We enjoy the ambience of our surroundings, and as the skies clear some of the mist lurking in the view between a couple of the huts, there arising in the distance between two tall trees is Kilimanjaro in all his glory. What an amazing sight, as if he has just crept up to have a view of his latest visitors. Most of what we can see is snow covered, a white mass standing out on the horizon. Clouds are still hovering around the lower slopes (that we can see).

Truly, truly spectacular, a view that I think will remain with me forever, and a view that will appear many times to me in the following few days. Spectacular, yet some miles away, but I suppose at its height, I expected it to look far taller. I wonder what Everest looks like at this distance with its extra ten thousand feet. But I would still have to say that it looks quite a climb, and not an easy one at that, it looks very steep at the top.

Our peace is disturbed by the arrival of what looks like another couple of walkers, probably just returning. They appear out of the reception area, make their way to their hut, and that's all we see of them. We have the pool to ourselves, and by now it is looking too tempting so I wander round to the steps, say hi to Jeff and Neil and enter the pool for a swim. It is pleasantly warm, and seems very fresh, so I do a few lengths, a couple underwater. It's good to stretch the muscles after the long journey and I feel all the better for it.

Having swam for a few minutes, I get out and sit on the steps in the shallow end of the pool. The other two have set up base here (so while I dry, and it is plenty warm enough just to dry in the sun), I chat with Neil and Jeff. Early, mid-forties, it turns out they went to school together in the Eastern counties, and have remained friends ever since. Neil works in sales, Jeff has just left the Army, tried his hand at one or two things, but basically is just looking for something that he will enjoy doing. One had rung the other up to see if he was up to the challenge of walking this mountain, and Neil had accepted the challenge. Neil is a keen triathlete, and this sort of challenge was right up his street. Jeff of course was used to the hard yards of army yomping. He was to extend his holiday when we had completed the climb, to fly on to Zanzibar for a few days. Again, it was getting to know each other, and time for another Kili beer; we supped by the pool for a little while.

They all seemed very pleasant, and strangely for a group of only five, three of us were hockey players, but we all did have the enjoyment of sport in common. It was nice to chat but it was also good then to sit back by the side of the pool, just switch off and read for a while. The waiters/waitresses were in constant attendance, very friendly but a little over attentive. But then, they had no-one else to wait on.

When Chunga and William had left us shortly after our arrival at the hotel, they said they would return at about five to give us a briefing about the climb and the next few days. They duly arrive back, and come into the pool area armed with folders, maps, etc., which they place on a table and draw up chairs around so that we can all sit around and hear them as they do their introduction. Orders are taken for beer, tea, and coffee for all of us, and then when we are all seated both Chunga and William introduce themselves formally to us, and explain their respective roles on the climb. Chunga is the tour leader, in general charge of everything – the camps, our wellbeing, organising the porters. William is the walk leader, so he will be in charge of the day-to-day trekking, leading us on that. He is reaching the stage where he has done enough hours and climbs to be assessed as to whether he can become a tour leader, and this process will take place on our trip, so we will have some say in his career progression.

We are shown on a map (which we can also purchase, surprise!) the route we will take up the mountain, and our starting point tomorrow. General information is given, the usual questionnaires about health, and also if any of us are medically trained, which technically I am. Chunga outlines the rough climb, the changes in scenery and climate we will see and what the different demands on clothing etc. will be as we go further into our expedition. Forest to moorland and then desert, and finally the ascent to the snow-covered summit, where we will be walking at night and the temperature will drop appreciably.

We have to undertake that he is in charge, and we will have to do what he says, and his is the final decision as to whether we as individuals will be able to proceed on the walk at any stage if he thinks that we are suffering medically, especially from altitude sickness. That is hard but we have to accept his authority for our own safety; people die on this mountain. So that is the serious part, and then just a run over the basic needs, about phone reception, whether cameras will work in the freezing temperatures above, about our experience of climbing and what we had done to train. That was all very different, and perhaps thinking before departure I hadn't done enough, it may be that I have done more than the others, though I am the eldest. Claire and Chris have done Everest Base Camp, and of course Jeff has done a lot in the army, but I have done most walking recently though I have no experience of altitude and cold.

Having gone through clothing requirements, Chunga says he will come and help us with our travelling luggage if required, and I accept his invitation as it is better to have it right than carry too much or too little. He has told us porters will be carrying our overnight stuff for us, we will just walk with food, water, extra clothing, waterproofs etc. if we think we will need them, and personal items such as cameras. The other thing that I hadn't considered was water purification tablets, as our water would be picked up en route out of mountain streams. Better to be safe than sorry, so it was better to add these tablets to water bottles as we refilled them. We are advised that we want to be carrying and drinking five to six litres a day – a lot – and I think my water bottles will carry about four, so I will have to make sure I drink plenty in camp, but yes, there will be a need for the purification tablets. Not a problem that I hadn't got any, Neil too – we would buy some in the morning as we went quickly to Chunga's office, and there was a shop nearby we could get them from. So all has been explained to us, and lastly there is the subject of tipping. The porters, and William as well, are paid by the operator company, but some of their wage will come as a tip from us, and there are scales of remuneration they should receive from a fund made up from the headage of climbers making the trip, in our case five. So it is agreed we will contribute $180 each, from which they will all receive something from. Chunga himself, doesn't come out of this, and it is up to us to decide how much we will reward him with when we are done. So that is all about sorted. Chunga says he will book a table in the hotel for us for seven to eat supper, and that in the morning after breakfast we will be picked up outside the reception of the hotel at eight o'clock, luggage ready, and we will begin. The only other consideration we were given was what to do on our return from the mountain. The Friday would be our final day on the mountain, our return flights back home on Saturday afternoon, so the possibilities on Saturday morning were: 1) relax at the hotel until it was time to depart from the hotel, 2) go into Moshi to shop and look round, or 3) to get up early and visit Arusha National Game Park, something I would like to do to see some of the African wildlife which had interested me for so long. Something to think about but no need to make a decision yet.

So now a bit more down time; the sun is going down so we leave the pool area, agreeing to meet just before seven so that we will eat our supper together. Back to the room, and I finish my laying out my kit, and put in piles clothing for different parts of the trip, and separate out my luggage which I will not take at all, some of which I have brought to leave for porters and their families. So, I think I am sorted, but as said earlier, Chunga said he would check, so I waited for him, and on his arrival went through what I had and what I thought I would take, which he thought was fine, but paying special attention to what I intended to wear for the final climb. All seemed okay so he departed with thanks, and wishing him farewell until the morning.

Time to use more of the hotel facilities, so a quick shower, although the workings of it took a bit of sorting out, a shave and then while drying off, sitting down for a few minutes, collecting myself together, and reading a few pages. I did start putting a few things into my holdall again, bedding at the bottom along with warm clothing that I definitely wasn't going to use tomorrow, or for a day or two I hope, and then as it neared seven, I left all this to finish after supper and the last few bits and pieces, when I get up in the morning.

I lock my room, descend my outside staircase and wander along the path to the reception area, meeting up with Chris and Claire on the way. We reach reception, where William and Chunga are still about, and wait there for the other two to come. They eventually do and we are shown through into the restaurant. At this time of day we have lost the sun and dark is fast approaching. How many staff do they have, all trying to busy themselves to please us? We are seated on a long table in the window. The temperature is still pleasant, as we are given menus and a while to make our choices. More drinks, and I would have to say this Kilimanjaro beer (more strictly lager) I am taking quite a liking to.

Having ordered, this is the first time the five of us have really been on our own, so now we have a chance to remove the barriers and start to try and get to know each other better. A brief introduction of each of us to the others, and then we can just chat generally, although we try to involve everyone in the conversation. A bit of piss taking amongst all, but already it would seem that Chris will be our leader, our voice (even if I do suspect it is Claire who wears the trousers). Jeff, being ex-army, is obviously a strong personality, and as we even touch politics, one can see that he and Chris will have to beg to differ on some things. But their chats on the regiment, and where in tight situations loyalties lie are interesting (a conversation that would be continued further down the line as we climbed, and descended).

So we gave our orders, not an exciting menu, but probably better to know what we are eating than risk a stomach upset on the first day of the walk. So for me, a basic tomato soup followed by chicken. We enjoy each other's company as we have our first course; that cleared away, then on to our main course. One problem, while the other five tucked into theirs with relish, mine, a non-appearance. I waited patiently, much to the others' amusement, but no, it wasn't coming, so had at last to enquire, and from the rapid actions in the kitchen which was fully visible from where we sat, it had been forgotten and was being cooked now, so when it did arrive, the others had already finished this course. A delay for them while I caught them up, conversation continued and pulling my leg about my meal. But all ends well and we move on to ordering our sweet, and sit back continuing our chat. Out of five of us, three of us are hockey players, three of us are Man United supporters and we are all rugby fans. Plenty in common, this is good, because we are going to be on top of each other for the next few days.

Sweets arrive, and we tuck in, except this time it is Neil's that doesn't arrive. Oh well, nothing goes smoothly. It comes eventually, we eat up, and enjoy a coffee together before turning in to rest for the start of our adventure.

Before this, we do have some confusion over the dinner

bill which they wanted us to pay, but as far as we were concerned we had already paid in our package, and said they should sort it all out with Chunga in the morning when he came back to pick us up. All was quite amenable, a slight misunderstanding, but one would have to congratulate the staff on their friendliness and willingness to help wherever they could. We all retired to our rooms in our lodges, wishing each other goodnight and agreeing to breakfast together at seven the following morning.

In my room, I finished my packing of my holdall, there would just be a few things to add to my rucksack for me to carry, and washing things to go with the porter luggage after washing in the morning. All done so, though not too late, at nine thirty, it's time for bed, and hopefully a good night's sleep, what I fear may be the last for a few days. The bed really is comfortable, but my mind is awash with thoughts as I am about to start my life's ambition.

So, before switching the light off, a few reflections on the story so far. This is the furthest south I have ever been. The climate today, pleasant, sunny, warm and with a gentle breeze. Very impressed with the view of the mountain behind us in the hotel grounds and it feels strangely as if Kilimanjaro has become my friend, my quest, and yes, I am in awe of this great mountain. I hope I am going to be treated well up there, tomorrow is another day and we will see how we get on.

The positives are that my climbing companions all seem very pleasant. It is strange now to think that only a couple of weeks ago, and me not knowing, it all could have been cancelled as with only three of us it was deemed too small a party. But luckily Chris and Claire signed up and here we all are.

So, here we are together and ready to start. The others are probably a bit fitter, but then they are younger, and they have done this sort of thing before to greater or lesser degrees. Me, the highest I had done was Snowdon twice, and of course duration-wise, that trek over Exmoor doing the Coleridge

Way a couple of months ago. Distance wouldn't be a problem, the altitude, I was about to find out. So, yes, at this stage I am apprehensive but excited, unsure but willing, and we can only see how I get on.

One thing is for sure, failure does not seem an option for the others. Me, I will try, and fingers crossed will succeed in my quest.

Only a couple of other thoughts; I hadn't expected the snow to be down the lower slopes so far, how difficult would this make walking, and how cold would it be? The other was my good old tum, which already had decided not to be in best form. I had given prior instructions, notice of my dairy intolerance, and what food we will get I am soon to find out. I hope it settles down quickly as toilet facilities will be at best, basic.

With that, it is time to put it all to the back of my mind and try and sleep. The night is peaceful, the mountain out of sight for the time being, and we all shall rest. Contented, I settle down in this wonderful room and I am at one with my world. Oh, and I put my phone on charge, that will be the last chance until we are back here again. How much I shall use, who knows!

Until the morning. Kilimanjaro awaits an audience.

9. WE ARE WALKING – LEMOSHO (2100M) TO BIG TREE CAMP (2780M)

JUNE 29TH 2012

Well almost, but we are not there yet.

Dawn arrives at the lodge, and I arise at six thirty. I would have to admit that I would have preferred a better night's sleep after the long journey, and the potential of no sleep for the next seven nights, but at least if fitful, I had managed some. Well, I can't change anything now, so I get up, make myself a coffee (a nice cup, and coffee is a locally grown product here), shower, shave (again may be the last time for a while), and finish my preparations. Decisions, what to wear to start the climb, with the great unknown of what the mountain has in store for us. I will risk shorts and a polo shirt today and see how I get on, and just put one or two extra layers in my rucksack so I have them if necessary. But with walking boots, I will wear proper thick walking socks from the off, I don't want to be getting blisters at the start of the trek. We will vacate our rooms when we leave for the start of the walk, but the hotel is quite happy to store our excess baggage in their storeroom until our return. So, having sorted this out, this can all go in a separate bag to be handed in. Not a lot more I can do now, so twiddle my fingers for a few minutes until seven o'clock, the time we said we would meet for breakfast together.

It's not a long walk to the restaurant, but dawn has come, a bit overcast, and at this stage our mountain has hidden himself in the clouds again. The temperature is pleasant, not excessively warm, but pleasantly comfortable. I am first in the lobby, but Claire and Chris soon follow, and not long after, the other two. We are the only ones down this early – not knowing what to expect on the climb, but soon to find out. Again, plenty of staff about waiting on us, and a vast array of food presented to us – fruit, cereals, toast, cold meats and a cooked breakfast. Well, do I ever refuse bacon? No. What the food will be like on the climb we don't know, so eat well as the opportunity arises, yes, a full cooked breakfast for me. The others tuck into cereal and fruit while I wait for mine to be cooked, they will have a cooked breakfast afterwards, and for me while I wait, a lovely cup of black coffee. My breakfast arrives, and is very good, though in preference I would have had the bacon cooked a little more, but it is good and will see me in good stead for the start of the day. A fruit juice to follow and I'm done. The others eat their cooked breakfast, but a habit forming, this time it is Jeff's that doesn't arrive. At last it does, we finish up and are all in good spirits, ready to get underway. The banter, friendly bickering, continues between Chris and Claire, all light hearted but I wonder how we will all get on with each other as the climb goes on. There would appear to be some competitive rivalry between Jeff and Neil, no doubt originating from school days and carrying on through life, but after twenty years of leaving school if they are still such good friends, then good luck to them.

Anyway, after a hearty breakfast for all, we leave the table and go to get ready to leave, though there is still some confusion about the food bill, which we insist should all be included in our holiday cost. Chunga will sort it out.

We will rendezvous outside the front lobby of the hotel at eight o'clock to depart. So first back to my gorgeous room. I could quite happily stay in the luxury of this for the duration. Normal daily habits, wash, clean teeth and a final packing of these items I have just used into my holdall, and then clear my room. Time to put my walking boots on, and to put away my comfortable slip-ons. With my three bags, it is down to reception, signing out and leaving the one bag there until our return. Chunga has arrived with William, and gives us each a strong envelope that we can put our valuables in and leave at his office, in their safe. We are done at the hotel, meals sorted, and I will look forward to our return and final night here.

I had wondered what happens to us if we suffer on the mountain, and have to return early, whether we come back here or are just put up in a local hostel, and also the cost if that happens, but enough, no negative thoughts to start the day.

Our transport awaits us outside the hotel, a long wheel base Land Rover, which picked us up yesterday from the airport, same driver. Our luggage is assembled in a heap, and now we have to get it all in the transport, plus Chunga and William's kit, and of course the seven of us plus driver. After a little arranging, we are sorted, some behind the seats, some in the gap between the seats, leaving room for us to scramble over if we need to get out, and some on the spare seat. We board, me right in the back, on the drivers' side, and at last we are ready for the off.

Like all trips, I just want to be there now, at the start of the trek, but we have a few things to do. First port of call will be to our Outfitters, the company we have to have to escort us up the mountain as unaccompanied climbing is forbidden, as it is for this company, Ashanti Tours, that Chunga and William work for. So it is back into Moshi, retracing our steps from yesterday back to the main road before turning east into town. First part of the journey along the main road, past small holdings on either side of the road, again with poor maize crops that look beyond redemption, large areas of cloth laid down beside huts, where I presume millet has been spread out to be dried and then crushed into flour. Over a couple of streams with fast flowing water, past a golf course which I didn't expect to see, though it may be more accurate to describe it as a few areas of short-mown cultivated grass amongst short scrub, and then into the outskirts of Moshi. Bungalows in fenced compounds, a bit more money and wealth here, and a lot of small roadside shops no bigger than a small hut, which looked as if they had a dozen or so bottles of drink to sell and that was their stall.

Off the main road and onto a side street, we drew up outside a compound, the offices of Ashanti, with automatic opening barricade gates, we enter and park outside. Only a short stop so no need for us to get off the Land Rover. Chunga and William go in to deposit our valuables in the safe, and to receive any last instructions from the operators. They are back and it is now on to our next stop, a trekker's shop where we do leave the transport; the important thing here is for Neil and I to get our water sterilisation tablets. Some problems with the Tanzanian currency, easier for Neil to pay for both of us and I will sort it out with him later. We are done and finally on our way out of town, retracing the route we have come in on, and heading west towards Arusha.

This is the main road, so a good road but busy with cars trucks, and quite a lot of large lorries, so although travelling at a reasonable speed, it is not easy to overtake. Small villages are passed through, with farmers, mainly the women, selling tomatoes at the sides of the road. This is better farmed land with vast maize plantations stretching into the distance, apparently state-run farms, so irrigated and a far better level of agriculture.

One more stop on this road; Chunga recommends we get some biscuits, nuts, snacks, whatever we fancy to nibble at while we are walking, to keep the energy levels up. I have my ginger biscuits and Kendal Mint Cake in my rucksack, but take his advice and acquire a couple of packets of sweet biscuits that Chunga recommends (but later find not really to my liking). The others do get nuts, which later on reflection, I wish I had. It would seem obvious that Chunga and his tours are regular visitors to this store, almost like a Spar or small Co-Op back home.

Back on our way, the sun has appeared now, although

behind us. We eventually turn off this road onto a smaller but still good quality road as we head more northerly now. We see a few goat herds, some sheep, and a few cattle being herded by young boys in the fields, and still a lot of maize. Along the side of the road are small habitations, huts surrounded by small enclosures, but the huts seem so small with little obvious signs of ventilation. I wonder how families live in this hot climate in these "ovens", I suppose this is the poverty which is much of Africa.

This is a good road and we make rapid progress; much of the traffic has now disappeared, aside from the occasional lorry which we overtake as we head into less populated lands. The flat plains which we have travelled over are now turning into more undulating vista, with forest in the distance. The land seems more arid, the level of farming diminishing, and we are heading into a wilderness. And then on my side of the Land Rover, out of the clouds appears Kilimanjaro, a lone mountain rising in the distance. The road starts to deteriorate, in some state of disrepair in places, road works in other places, and it turns more into a dirt track, wide but very rutted in places and very dusty. Any thoughts of closing my eyes for a rest are spoilt by the constant banging of my head against the window as we hit another bump. The mountain appears no nearer as we continue along this "road".

And then we start to climb; the road improves as it becomes more windy. The sun has gone again now as we head into forested land, with a lot more people about, working the land. These are areas where courgettes, potatoes, and peas are being grown, on what seems far more fertile land. I presume this is reclaimed from forest, and with the temperatures here, and the humidity from its closeness to the rainforests, creates ideal growing conditions. We also start to see forestry working and a lot of logging, with stacks of processed trunks lying beside the road in organised piles. Again, we are told there is some state intervention in the cultivation of this area, organising the local labour to generate a more productive economy.

We wind upwards along this road, seeing more and more people, and at last reach some large gates, our next destination – Londorossi Gate. A large compound with many Africans waiting outside the gates, these apparently hoping they will be chosen as porters by one Outfitter or another to carry our luggage and camp equipment up the mountain for us. This is an important part in their financial stability, in that if they can get onto this work, it will greatly supplement their income, and is the bottom rung of a ladder which will eventually take them to a well-paid job as Tour Leader such as Chunga has, and William after this trip will hope to attain.

We park up in the compound where there are a few small trucks, and a hut. Is this our starting point in the clouds? Dull and no sign of the sun now, but from one place, the peak of Kili can be seen in the distance still, to the east. The cloud is increasing though. We have travelled some eighty kilometres from our hotel to here, across varying qualities of road, but we are here ready to start.

Chunga and William meet up with old friends, a lot of good banter between comrades they have seen before and presumably done this trek with before. A crew needs to be chosen to accompany us, and it seems to some extent that this has already been done, so despite the pleas from the people at the gate, our camp leader, cook, his assistants, and porters are already organised, and getting our "camp" organised and loaded – we still have further to go.

For our part, as do all climbers on the mountain, we have to go to the hut and register as a party, names, age, nationality etc., something which we will have to do several times on our travels over the next few days. This doesn't take very long, and as we complete this process, we are given a plastic box each, this containing today's lunch. They seem to think unfortunately that I am a vegetarian, so mine is quite boring, some weird cheesy things (of course one of the things I am not supposed to eat), cakes, and a chocolate bar. There is a proper loo here as well, the last we will see for a while, so we use the facilities while they are available, and then have a nibble at our lunch pack while they finish loading all we will need for the expedition. They do this with much noise and frivolity, and are eventually done.

We get back in the Land Rover, and are ready to go, with a lorry bringing the rest of the camp equipment. We even have a couple of porters climb on top of the Land Rover, their seat for the journey to the start of the walk proper. Precarious, more so as we will find out in a short while. By now, Kili has disappeared out of sight, but we can see Meru to our south-west. We pass back through the gates, still with many men waiting patiently for their chance to do the climb as porters, some old hands, some very young. What an important part of their economy the mountain must bring to take them out of poverty to some extent, supplementing their basic income from the land, and allowing them to improve their way of life; better housing and all that follows.

We head back down the way we have come, winding back down the road for a while before turning off to the left and passing through a conifer plantation. Our first sighting of any wildlife, there sitting high in the conifers, are a group of Columbus monkeys. Wonderful-looking New World monkeys, quite happily sitting high up branches, watching us from a distance. Apparently they only have four digits on their hands. We stop to watch them for a few minutes, them, minding their own business. For those who it is easy to get out of the Land Rover, they get out to take a few photographs. From my position, it is easier to stay where I am and try and picture them through the windows. A wonderful sight indeed, beautiful creatures.

Time to move on, so all aboard again and we continue through the forest. It's still dull and cloudy, and beneath the forest canopy amongst the trees, in the surrounding open land we see many Tanzanians working the soil, again very fertile-looking, the same crops as before, and presumably extending into the forest as far as there is natural light, essential for the healthy growth of their crops. French beans seem to be grown here in plenty as well. This is very good use of land which we don't see back in Britain, though I suppose most forest areas back home tend to be on poorer soil areas.

The road now can only best be described as a track, getting rougher and rougher as it gets more and more rutted. We would be a few weeks after the big rains, so muddy as well in places. So the journey slows; I wonder how our friends on the roof are getting on, they sound happy. We continue along, passing more workers in the fields, cultivating, weeding, getting on with their daily tasks, but then unfortunately meet a logging lorry blocking our track. A real squeeze to get past this one, as to some extent our course is governed by the ruts, but we do get by.

The ruts are getting worse and worse, deeper and deeper, and at some stages we are driving really tilted over, the window by where I am seated almost touching the muddy banks we are at such an angle. We can't go much further than this, and we reach a point where Chunga and the driver decide enough is enough, so on finding a clearing where we can stop and turn round, that is it, the walk starts from here, a bit short of where we were supposed to be dropped off. Never mind, it is a walking holiday that we have chosen. It will apparently put an extra mile on the walk.

So, here we stop, unload the jeep and await the arrival of the lorry carrying the other porters, camp equipment, etc. Chunga can keep in regular contact with them by walkie-talkie, but of course they have the same trip as us, the same ruts, and the same possible obstructions on the way. The clean Land Rover that picked us up earlier, is now filthy, especially on my side where we had rubbed up against the banks on the side of the track when at our most tilted. But well done to our driver for getting us this far.

While we wait for the lorry we finish off our packed lunches, I'm glad I had the cooked breakfast as I'm not enjoying this very much, and the chocolate has a very strange taste, not that pleasant. A call of nature and wandering away from the others for a bit of privacy, what is in front of me, can't escape from good old stinging nettles, except these are far bigger than our British versions, and Chunga says, will cause a lot of irritation.

It's one o'clock, the day seems to be dragging, and from their radio contact it is obvious that the lorry is still going to be a little time in arrival, held up by the same loggers as us but their vehicle is wider so passage is not straight forward. It is decided that we will start on our way, we are off, so on go the rucksacks. We sort out gaiters to try and keep cleaner, and at last we are underway. William explains to us that the important thing to get used to now, even more so as we get to higher altitude, is our speed of walking. Oxygen will get thinner the greater the altitude, so we start at the pace he requires of us the higher we get. "Pole, pole" (slow/slow) is the pace, and we must get used to this as we set off in single file along the wet and muddy path. It seems very pedestrian, but it will keep us together and stand us in good order in later days to come. It is obvious that the vehicles couldn't have come any further down the path than where we were dropped off.

We walk quietly to begin with behind William, as we get used to his pace. It is a gentle slope at this stage as we start walking through the edges of the rainforest, easy going, and as we adjust to pole, pole we start to relax more and start chatting amongst ourselves, getting to know each other better. I take up a position in the middle of the party, usually third in line; it's not a race so at the moment the competitive streak has gone from our younger men.

We reach a clearing, surrounded by very tall trees; what flowers there are, are also very tall. This is where the walk would have begun if we had been able to reach it by vehicle,

Lemosho Glade, a distance of about eleven kilometres from Londorossi Gate, but for one reason or another, had taken us a little longer than was reckoned.

The flora seem very similar to what I expect to see in woodland at home, just a lot taller, geraniums, cow parsley, etc. What does surprise me is that the forest is a lot more sparse in the number of trees than I expected, and the absence of the vast amount of lichens that I expected to be hanging from them. More like a few trees growing tall on the surrounding slopes, each trying to find its own light. And far quieter than I had expected, not the chatter of birds all the time, just the occasional song. And where is the sun? But it is a comfortable walking temperature.

We start the walk proper from Lemosho Glade, about another three hours' walking as we make our way to our first overnight stop. This is classed as a gentle day's walking. So again in single file, on we go. The porters will catch us up and overtake us so that by the time we reach camp, tents will be put up and our campsite organised. We are loosening up, and though we start to ascend on a narrowing path which requires some concentration, we start to chat more amongst ourselves. Chris and Jeff are the obvious talkers; Chris seems to have a story about most things, and Jeff's army life has meant he has a broad knowledge of the world. Claire and Chris seem to have a wonderful bickering relationship, he is obviously highly thought of by Claire's family and has acquired the name "Tosser 2". Her parents are apparently farmers near Hereford so we have something else in common. Chris being a rugby correspondent is also very interesting, and as said earlier, he had just returned from England's brief tour to South Africa. And with the three hockey players we have a lot in common, and so should have plenty to chat about while we are walking, and should all be able to interact together. William walks in front, Chunga in the rear to keep an eye on us, every now and again catching us all up to see how we are doing. We have frequent stops for water. We are instructed to carry three litres a day when walking, which in turn means the occasional call of nature, more difficult for our lady to disappear into the bushes, but at every necessary stop, Chunga would hang back to make sure we were okay and joined the group again.

The path continues to wind upwards, some gentle slopes, some more steep, but on we go, damp and muddy in places, and slippery too from time to time. To our left in places, the slope falls rapidly away into tree lined valleys. We stop at one point to watch a trail of soldier ants crossing our path, thousands and thousands of them forming a line some five centimetres across, all intent on a common purpose in one direction. We take great care not to interfere in their passage; Chunga warns us that any bite, and there would be many if we were to be attacked, would be more than extreme discomfort as they bite into flesh. The wonders of nature.

As we continue to climb, we are eventually caught and overtaken by groups of porters from time to time, carrying their loads on their heads but leaving us behind for pace. I suppose they are used to the altitude and are far fitter than us, they certainly don't carry any excess pounds. William tells us the local greeting, "Jambo", which they appreciate as they pass us, a sign we respect them and in time we will pick up more words of the local language. So as they pass us, we all greet them with "Jambo," and they return the greeting to us. A basic hello and they always reply with a big smile on their faces. By the time we reach camp they will have been there a little while, and got the camp erected for us, theirs and our tents, the kitchen and dining tents, and started to prepare a meal.

We carry on climbing and in places it is getting very slippery, making it hard work, not helped by tree roots crossing the path frequently meaning you had to find your footing carefully. This meant some scrambling was needed as well. In one place, single file, we scramble over a concoction of roots and very undulating earth, slippery underfoot. Chris is walking behind me, and unbeknown to me loses his footing, falling forwards, nearly knocking me over as well. I manage to stay on my feet, Chris, not so lucky as he falls and becomes covered in mud. This is much to Claire's amusement as she calls out "Tosser!" to him. Checking Chris is okay, and helping him to his feet, we carry on.

Further up the route, we have swopped places, with Chris now in front of me. It gets muddy again and as he climbs he slips again, this time falling backwards – and nearly fells me again. We laugh and carry on, on our path upwards. At this stage of the walk, all bar me were using walking poles, I had them but had never used them before, and was happy to have my hands free to steady myself in case I slipped.

The slope steepens, and we move to the side of the path to allow two armed Tanzanians to pass us, carrying rapid-fire rifles. Why? We wonder. Security or danger? On we go. We have been going for a good couple of hours, and just is becoming a common word; we will stop in just a minute, just a little further, just round the next bend, but always it's a bit further we go. At last we are told the camp is just round the corner, and as we turn the bend the forest, which is quite dense here, it opens into a large clearing, with a few trees still standing in it, a wooden hut, and there is our camp being set up in front of us.

Big Tree Camp is our first introduction to what life will be like. The porters are busying themselves, the tents, toilet tents which are apparently a rare luxury for climbing parties, but provided as we have a lady on board. To the left of the camp in some tall trees we get to see the first animals we have encountered since walking, some more Columbus monkeys. I really thought we would have seen more forest life, more monkeys and especially birds (larger mammals do apparently inhabit the forested slopes of the mountain, but often remain concealed amongst the trees and shrubs, some as large as buffalo). How graceful these monkeys seem, gliding through the trees, tranquil and taking no notice of our invasion into their privacy.

Big Tree Camp (locally known as Mti Mkubwa, but the computer doesn't seem to recognise these words!) is our first camp. The hut is a ranger's hut, but not occupied on our visit, and our base is to the right edge of the clearing, tents erected, our luggage arranged in a heap by the tents, and past that two wooden huts which we learn are drop-down toilets, something we will become much acquainted with over the next few days as we go from one camp to the next. We are allocated our tents, obviously paired as before which means I have one to myself. We then find our kit and start to organise ourselves in our five-star accommodation. We are on the edge of the campsite, another three or four yards and we are back in forest. Not far away is a large fallen tree lying on the forest floor. We are busying ourselves quietly, when out of the forest onto this fallen tree emerges a large monkey, walking on all fours, stopping on the trunk and then staring at us for some time. A magnificent animal, about the size of a small Labrador, he just sits and stares as if he knows there is food to his liking in the camp. I manage to get a couple of decent photos, before a crowd gathers, when he thinks enough is enough and he moves on down the trunk, onto the forest path and continues on his journey. One last look back at us, raising himself onto just his back feet, he is so tall; no food here for the time being and he is gone, wandering back into the forest.

Excitement over, we have a little down time to organise ourselves before supper and getting used to camp routine. Our mess tent has been erected so we do have a chance of a tea break, biscuits etc. served in our "canteen". Keep the fluid levels up – very refreshing and a quick chance to reflect on the walk so far.

Other parties are arriving in the campsite, and at one time a group of porters form a guard of honour, singing an African song as a group come into camp. Americans it turns out, one guy is absolutely massive, and helping escort a double amputee walking into camp. Amazing how he would have managed some of that terrain, hard enough for us able bodied, and one has to admire the courage and determination of some people to reach their goals. I think I read just before I departed on this holiday, that somebody had ascended the mountain in a wheelchair.

Back to my tent, and time to try and organise my bedding. The first time I had inflated the mattress; not that thick so how comfortable I will be I don't know, then I organise the sleeping bag, its fleece inner liner and pillow. I hope it will provide enough comfort for at least restful sleep. Other than washing stuff, not much else needs organising but I am as organised now as I need to be.

It doesn't seem long since our tea break, but supper is ready. A bowl of hot water and soap is provided by our faithful support, so we can wash before the meal. We gather again in our canteen, perched around our dining table, on not very comfortable or stable chairs. Chunga joins us as he will for every evening meal. I am perched the far side of the table, facing outwards through the tent doors. As we are seated, our friend the Blue Monkey, reappears on the fallen log on the edge of the camp. Those closest to the door pile out for a better view, and to get more photos. I try and get my camera out of the camera case on my belt in anticipation of a shot, but realise I am not going to get out in time before he starts to wander off again. He disappears back into the forest, the moment gone, and we all return to our seats. It is six thirty.

A hearty supper is served to us, no individual treatment, just six plates, bowls, whatever, and the meal is put in the middle of the table, help yourself. A first course of soup, not bad, followed by stew and two veg and lastly fruit to finish. It has been a long and varied day, and we all eat well, before finishing the meal with tea or coffee. We carry on talking, small talk, joking and finding out about each other. Chunga tells us of tomorrow's journey, our daily briefing session where we are told to be up at six thirty, wash and have breakfast then prepare to move on, onwards through the forest and then onto the Shira Plateau. It transpires the men armed with rifles who had passed us on the climb were for our protection – the odd marauding buffalo had been known to wander into camp and cause havoc.

The theme of Tosser 2 continues to come up. Chris is in the centre of most conversations, and I slowly come out of myself, joining in more, especially on the subject of older single men, as Jeff is too now, and that if you went to the right places it was not difficult to meet up with other like-minded people looking for company or more. I worried they may think me the local lothario of Shropshire, but it's all a good laugh.

Dark comes quickly in Africa, as I found in Egypt when you could time the setting of the sun in minutes. And as the light went, even being so close to the Equator, the temperature dropped rapidly as well to the extent we were going to the tents to get fleeces to keep warm. By eight thirty it was noticeably cold and time to call it a day.

Torch light was our source of navigation, which wasn't going to be more than using the facilities before settling down in our tents to read by torchlight or just settle straight down. Unlike the other parties, we did have our portaloo which was placed handily just away from our tents. Primarily because of Claire; she will get priority in a rush while we have the drop down toilets available. So I stagger over guy ropes up the path to one of these. As I adjust myself, I hear a clunk in the dark, and realise it is my camera which I can't have replaced properly in its pouch. There was a concrete standing which we "aimed" downwards from into the depths of, well you can imagine. I cannot feel anything in the dark, and fear the camera has fallen into the pit. I go to get a torch, bumping into Claire on the way down. We scour the hole and below for a sighting of it, and there laying on the surface of the s—t is, yes, my camera.

Claire suggests I find Chunga and explain what has

happened, they may be able to do something. He is not in his tent but the porters find him for me, and he bravely says they can rescue it for me. Me, I am not so hopeful, and doubt if their plan will work. However/, they rig up some device they have which will extend into the depths, and eventually manage to hook the string of the camera handle. Slowly but surely, inch by inch lifting it out of the s—t until it emerges above the concrete rim. They are really pleased with themselves to retrieve it, and of their success. I find a toilet roll to clean the camera with, and they go about this task with a smile on their faces. Satisfied, they return the camera to me. What wonderful people, so friendly, happy and helpful. I thank them and return to my tent, it's ten past ten and now very cold.

I snuggle into my fleece inside my sleeping bag and try to arrange myself in a position where I will get a degree of comfort, then try to settle down.

But, after the excitement, the start of the walk, the climb and everything else in the day, the events of the past couple of hours have made me feel more than a bit down. An African dream, which I wanted to record, now in tatters, literally down the pan (the camera at this stage didn't seem that interested in living. I placed it in a plastic bag within my sleeping bag in the hope that body heat would dry it out a little). My confidence, slow in coming, to reach my goal of climbing to the top of Kilimanjaro had plunged as if fate said it would not happen. I feel low as I snuggle down in my sleeping bag in thermal vest and pants.

The walking so far, not too bad, climbing from 2100 metres to 2780 metres, a walk of about three and a half hours, and the highest I have ever been. The company I now share with my new colleagues is good but because of the camera, my morale is low.

We will see what tomorrow brings.

10. BIG TREE CAMP TO SHIRA CAMP 1

JUNE 30TH

My first night under canvas is over at just under 2800 metres. Having eventually snuggled down in my sleeping bag at just gone ten o'clock, from the tog values of it and the fleece lining, I had expected to be warm and so other than vest and pants, had not worn anything else. After the traumas of the evening it was always going to be difficult to settle – and I didn't.

It was a restless night and I couldn't get comfortable, and I was cold – very cold. The ground was hard, despite the mattress, so I tossed and turned all night, snuggling into as small a ball as I could to try and keep warm. And of course, the calls of nature – I must remember in future not to drink too much at night close to bedtime, and that after I went to bed a couple of hours later than I had intended. Getting a few clothes on by torch light is not easy, I wonder how many of the others have made this trip in the dark. The zips to the tent are a real challenge too, a two-handed job when you need one to hold the torch (more of that later). Then dodging guy ropes of the others' tents – I don't want to crash in on them, literally, as they are sleeping, and then the loo tent (I'm not risking the drop downs again in the dark!), more ropes, another zip, and then when finished, how to flush the damn thing. Then reverse the process, more zips, and then crawling back into the sleeping bag, and trying then to sleep again. I think I heard one other trying the trip.

Sleep doesn't come, and by six o'clock I am busy

watching the clock waiting for our early morning call, to be up for breakfast by six thirty and on our way by seven thirty. A knock on the door, well, a tap on the tent, slight unzipping and a question of coffee or tea, the porter, second cook as he is, is surprised that I am waiting for him. Having gone round the others, he soon re-emerges with my cup of black coffee. A smiling face and so early in the morning. I am up and dress while drinking my coffee, and of course all this has to be done kneeling or sitting as the tents are low.

It is light outside now as the forest awakens with the noise of birds and Columbus monkeys, as I have seen described as the sounds of a quintessential African dawn, whatever that means, to me the sounds of the forest starting its day. This is how the day will start while on the mountain, without the sounds of the forest. Having dressed, I start to repack my bedding and deflate the mattress, being warmed by that most welcome cup of coffee. Packing the sleeping bag, the mattress will become easier as we progress and I get into a routine of getting the air out quickly and managing to roll them as small as they will go to get them back in the holdall easily.

Hot water is provided outside for us, a couple of enamel bowls to wash in with soap again. Leaving the tent to have a wash and a shave, it looks as if I am the only person bothering to shave. I finish getting dressed, finish the last of the coffee, and our breakfast is ready.

What will we get now we are on the walk? We assemble in the mess tent again, and Chunga joins us for our meal. A big bowl of porridge arrives, and this is most welcome as we have been so cold. Chatting amongst ourselves, it seems I wasn't the only one who was cold, though the others had the advantage of two in a tent to provide each other with a bit more body heat. It was Chris that I had heard in the middle of the night, Jeff and Neil had slept well. The porridge goes down well, and this is followed by a cooked breakfast, frankfurters, fried eggs, and beans (these not for me though). And a ready supply of bread, tea and coffee. We don't see the cook who is feeding us royally, presumably cooking on just a couple of campus stoves, but we have a loyal waiter who will bring us all our food over the trip, and is our early morning call.

Chunga tells us about the day to come and what to expect, a trip out of the forest onto moorland as we head towards the Shira Plateau, and of course gaining altitude as we go. Sounds an interesting, and quite a long day. Obviously by now, everyone knows about my camera, and although I am upset about it, have to take the banter, the laughs are on me. Am I Tosser 3?

Breakfast was good though, and that routine would follow every day. As we rose from the table, packed lunches were handed out once again, the same as yesterday so I'm still a vegetarian despite them watching me eat stew last night. Yippee, something for me to look forward to later. Back outside the tent, the most important job, refill the water bottles, add the sterilisation tablets, and pack them in my rucksack. Then, finish packing my rucksack, along with the camera to see what crap pictures I may be able to take. At the moment, the screen is a bit blurred like some liquid has got in the workings, though not quite as bad as last night. I will put it somewhere warm and hope it continues to dry. Then pack the kitbag with what is left, and get it outside so our friends can start dismantling the tent, and pack up the camp. We put the kit in a pile, which they will take on to the next camp for us.

The sun is starting to shine, giving a little warmth through the forest canopy, but there is still a nip in the air. Clothes wise, I start with my thermal vest, shirt, jumper and fleece, shorts again, walking socks – then with water, nibbles, my camera, a waterproof and the packed lunch in the rucksack, I have plenty of room to put clothes in if I take them off on route.

After assembling, we set off on the next part of our adventure. In places there is frost on the ground, but above us through the canopy of leaves, the sun shines in a glorious blue sky. We are on the move, leaving on time just after seven thirty, on a well-worn path, and starting to climb already between the trees. It is quite a long walk today, and altitude may start to cause problems a little further on, so pole, pole is the order again, a slow, step-by-step approach. We hear the occasional bird, but otherwise it is very peaceful, and this is a glorious, attractive forest so it is nice just to savour our surroundings and the forest atmosphere.

My camera is still a source of amusement, but both Jeff and Claire say if there is anything I would like a picture of, then just tell them and they will take it, and on our return will forward the photos to me. This is really kind of them, much appreciated, though I don't feel I can keep saying "Stop, take this or this," but in expressing my gratitude, I say that if I can just have a selection of theirs unless there is anything I really want. I do have my camera on my phone, but how long the battery is good for I don't know. Of course, my own camera may return to use, but on that I can only wait and see. I am not hopeful.

Conversation soon starts again, Chris and Jeff on their experiences in life as they are much travelled. Claire, I find out, is a farmer's daughter and being from the Marches, our conversation turns to tuberculosis in cattle, me as a vet being on the front line as it were, in our ever-worsening situation in Shropshire. The proposed badger cull comes up, my views, her views, and of course it is good to get other people's perspective on the subject.

Our journey progresses upwards, it is getting warmer but we still see the occasional frost-covered foliage. For a rainforest, this all seems very much like an English woodland, other than the height of the trees, and plants. Regular water breaks, sippi, sippi, are taken and very important. For most of us, popping behind a bush is easy when necessary, but not so for Claire who is more discreet, but Chunga will still be close by for our protection and escorting us safely back to the group when we are done.

After an hour or so, we can hear voices behind us, and the porters, having packed up the camp are now climbing fast onto our next stop, carrying everything on their heads, as they travel at a far faster pace than us. They are used to the lower oxygen levels in the air and are acclimatised to it. As they near, we step aside to let them pass with a smile and "Jambo." My friends from last night enquire about the camera and I can only thank them and say it is drying out so we will have to wait and see. Then they are gone and we continue our journey, climbing steadily, but not the steepness we encountered yesterday, nor the paths being so slippery.

As we climb, the trees are starting to thin, and this is a lovely walk as far as I am concerned. More flowers are to be seen, and without such a thick canopy above, they are not fighting for light so are smaller than encountered before. We seem to be walking along a ridge, and to our left the ground drops away, some gullies, and a few streams flowing gently down them. This is nearing the edge of the rain forest, and as I said yesterday, not quite what I was expecting, but this part is beautiful.

And then we are out into bright sunshine. The forest ends so abruptly that the change in vegetation is remarkable. We are now walking along a well-used path surrounded by heathers, some seven to eight feet tall, towering above us. We are now viewing a moorland landscape, and with that, the path becomes more and more rocky and we have to watch out for bare roots again, waiting to trip us up. Large boulders also appear – this is my Exmoor but on a grander scale. The forest finishes at about 3000 metres, and I really enjoyed the trek through it, but that is now the last cover we shall have until we are halfway down the mountain on our descent. But this is spectacular too, and with a beautiful, azure sky above, what could be better?

The path is steeper now, going up and down below the African sky, and it is now getting a lot hotter. We are starting to meet other walking parties as well; we are not the only people on this route, and of course the regular procession of their porters making their way in the same direction as us but at their own faster speed. As we travel along this well-trodden path, down into a small valley with a stream running through it, it was planned we would stop here for a break and get something to eat from our packs, but it looks like others have already thought to do this, so although it is a lovely spot, William decides we will go a little further. In places, the heather is not so tall, or there is more of a rocky clearing, and at one of these, looking to our left we can see Mount Meru, standing in the distance, its 4562 metres reaching into the clear skies. In front, the lower slopes of forest we have just climbed through forming a skirt around the lower slopes of Kili, and then stretching into the distance, the African plains. This is truly a memorable sight, and how I wish I had my camera for this. The scenery is stunning and it is now getting very warm so the layers are coming off, sunglasses go on, and some suntan lotion. This is exhilarating, and so far the walking easy. In these temperatures stops are becoming more frequent to drink water. We descend down into a dried river bed in a valley and then probably our hardest walk so far as we have to ascend up the other side of the valley which is rocky, steep and narrow, as we climb to reach a ridge at the top. There are large steps upwards, finding your footing on rocky ledges, making it a long hard climb but after some thirty minutes we reach the top, and what magnificent views from here.

We bear right, eastward, along this ridge, still climbing but a far gentler slope, along a narrow dirt path, skirting shrubs, bushes, and large rocks. Slowly up and up we go, 3500 metres, then another 100 metres. And then what we have been waiting for, because the last part has been hard. William calls us to a halt for lunch where there are two large, flat rocks that we can spread out on, not hindering any other walkers, and where we can take in the fantastic views around us. To our right, the ground falls steeply away from our rocky ledge, down into the valley we have just come out of. To our left, the path and a gentler slope falls away from us.

It is not quite midday, so time has flown as we have been walking for four hours, but it doesn't seem like it. We get out our lunches, but I can't say I am enjoying mine. I have been given a couple of chicken legs today, but again the cakes and the chocolate are not to my taste. Perhaps the wildlife will enjoy them more than me. There are a lot of flies here, even at this altitude, hovering about us, annoying, but thankfully not biting us. A picnic lunch beneath the African sun.

Our forty-minute lunch break, now over, but enjoyable in the sunshine, and very hot as well. Then we are off again, continuing up the ridge. There is a steady stream of people in front of us snaking their way up the ridge, mainly porters from different parties, making the climb look easy, with their loads on their head. We are told the camp is just over the other side of the crest of the ridge that we can see in the distance, that good old saying when you are walking, just over the next hill. It is all uphill at the moment as we head northwards to the edge of the Shira Ridge. The clouds start to roll in and the sky darkens from the west behind us. Are we going to get a storm? Nice that it is not so warm, but I don't want to get wet, not yet anyway!

So, after many false dawns, we reach the top of the ridge, and there in front of us is the vast openness of the Shira Plateau. Straight in front of us in the distance are the odd specks of tents and huts, Shira Campsite. Stretching out to our right along the ridge, one or two peaks along the Shira Hills, Shira Cathedral and Shira Cone. And most noticeably rising out of the plateau beyond the campsite, way in the distance is what we have come for – Kilimanjaro himself standing proud though the summit now hidden in the clouds. We can see the snow-covered slopes, some of the Western Breach, Lava Rock, and a vast emptiness between us and there. To our left we see the occasional stream of dust arising in the air, a track which goes to one of the other campsites, Shira 2, on this side of the mountain. It is the last place that can be reached by jeeps, which are creating the dust clouds in the distance. We are now at some 3800 metres above sea level, where altitude sickness can start to affect you, but for the rest of our walk today, we will be losing a little altitude again. Looking down on this moorland terrain, this really could be Exmoor, but on a grander scale.

The heather doesn't stand so tall above us now so our view is unimpeded as we start to descend towards the plateau, I guess another hour to walk. Chunga is in close proximity, so I chat to him about the wildlife found here. Yes, they do get elephants and buffalo here but not that often, some eland, small antelopes, dik dik, and impala. Disappointingly for my love of African wildlife, all I see is the calling card of jackal, after smaller prey.

Jeff gives us a running commentary on our altitude, with a clever device on his watch, and as we carry on down this narrow path, Chris just in front of me manages to stumble over another rock, falling sideways, only saved from a bad fall by a large heather he falls on top of, but again nearly bringing me down in the process. We drag him to his feet and reacquaint him with his walking poles; he is slightly scratched but nothing more serious. A little shaken, we rest up for a few minutes. We could do with a drink anyway, and then continue downwards until we reach the plateau floor, with a fairly level walk to the campsite. We finally arrive there at about three in the afternoon, where our camp has been set up by the porters at the far end of the site, past the huts which look a bit dilapidated. A well-made clearing in the heather with the odd large boulder laying around, and on the mountain side of the site, a large stream.

As we will find every day, our camp is already set out, our tents erected, the kitchen tent up and our cook already beavering away in there. Our kitbags are arranged tidily outside, and the loo tent is on the edge of the camp, out of everyone else's way.

The sun reappears – making this a lovely spot. The stream is surrounded with some bush, but accessible, only spoilt by the amount of litter that has been left lying about close to it. What a shame to spoil nature in this way. Again as we will find to be the norm each day at the end of our hike, the water bowls appear, plus hot water and soap, and after a wash our faithful friend appears with tea or coffee for us to refresh our thirsts.

Wash, then organise our tents once again, trying to think of different ways to try and gain some comfort and warmth for later on the hard plateau floor. Having done this, I shall try to make use of my Puffa jacket and waterproof to make my head more comfortable, but now it is time to go and enjoy the scenery. Neil, Jeff and I wander down to the stream for a look, and after the rigours of the day, they decide to go in for a dip. This is a mountain stream at 3500 metres, so for me no way – far too cold. The others are more hardy than me, and go in, deep enough in places for a splash around and a swim. Unfortunately their bravery is foreshortened by the porters who are not keen for them to be in there, there is a lot of metal rubbish in the stream, and as it transpires, this is our drinking water for the next day or two, as it is one of the last streams with water that we will see until...

After a little relaxation and reading in the sunshine, we are all called together, ourselves, the cooks, camp leader, all the porters, Chunga, and William. This is our formal introduction to our crew, so one by one we are introduced to them, and then them to us. Here, if I have one regret, and it is obvious in my text, I wish I could remember their names because as we would find out more and more over the next few days, they are truly wonderful people. At this stage all I can remember is Peter, the camp leader, the organiser who got everything done, shifted, taken up, taken down, and generally ran everyone else bar Chunga and William, but he would always be in radio contact with them. A hard-looking man, from his looks, not one I would want to cross, but dressed in his Aston Villa shirt, he was apparently some sort of priest. Later, I would be very grateful to him.

We were then given a Tanzanian welcome led by William. In unison they sing us a song similar to the American party received upon their arrival at Big Tree Camp yesterday, a song about Kili apparently. And then we are expected to return the welcome in song, how useless we are in that all we can do is a few renditions of the songs emanating from the terraces at Old Trafford. Luckily, Chunga, William and some of the others are United supporters. We shake hands with each other. They are so friendly and can't do enough for us, with enquiries about my camera, and then we break up so they can get back to their jobs of preparing our supper. I do take the opportunity of saying that I am not a vegetarian, I just can't eat dairy products.

The sun is still shining and the campsite is busying itself as more groups arrive, including our Americans. I sit outside and enjoy the weather while reading my book, though I am finding it hard going. Then it is supper again, and we reconvene in the mess tent with Chunga. We start with carrot soup (that should help if we need to find the loo tonight), and very good it is too. Then we are served up chicken casserole. We will take it in turn to be "mother" as the journey goes on, but already we are looking after each other.

We relate the day to each other Chris's fall. "Tosser," do I hear Claire say? And Chunga tells us of the day to follow, as we tuck into mango. Chunga certainly seems to like his fruit. He is very pleased with us as a group, the way we are getting on with each other and mixing well. Tomorrow we will walk to Moir Camp, a fairly steady but long walk with little change in altitude, and then after a rest, we would go on an acclimatisation walk up to the Lent Hills, which would be harder, then back to camp. We have hot drinks and the conversation continues on. It is here that Chris, not backward in coming forward, relates how back at Heathrow, he had seen these two blokes who looked as if they were doing this trip, and how he thought they looked more than good friends! Here they are sitting in front of us now. No offence is taken, and we have a good laugh over it, but I keep my counsel that back at Heathrow exactly the same thoughts had crossed my mind.

It is now getting appreciably colder, the sun is gone and we are under the clear, dark African night, the sky intermingled with stars shining brightly. And just silhouetted in the distance but creeping closer is Kilimanjaro. Eight o'clock, and time to turn in to try to keep warm, and to sleep.

So how am I doing? Today we walked for some seven hours including breaks, ascending from 2780 metres to 3500 metres. Walking in the most part is fairly easy, no problems with altitude sickness yet and I have coped with the heat, and despite the camera incident still playing on my mind (I had tried a few pictures but there were fluid lines on the screen so not looking good) I feel okay. I am getting a bit of light hearted ribbing about the camera, but we are all joking with each other, and seem to be settling into each other's company very well. At least I can get some of Jeff and Claire's photos when we return. We have had closer contact with our porters, who as I have already said are wonderful, and the food is very good.

I have enjoyed today, and am now settled in what by the end of the trip, in my opinion is the nicest of our campsites. Yes, I feel good and a bit of confidence is at last appearing, I am going to do it.

Early to bed means nights are long and cold, and my biggest concern now is comfort and sleep, or lack of. We will see what the morrow brings, but the mountain is now in our sight, and will only get closer.

Lunch and the walk begins.

Emerging from the rain forest towards Shira.

Columbus monkeys, a rare view of wildlife. Lemosho Glade.

A blue monkey at Big Tree Camp.

The team (less Claire taking the photo).

Chunga and some of our porters, William second from left.

The trek ahead, Kili slowly gets closer.

The Kilimanjaro ambulance.

11. SHIRA CAMP TO MOIR HUT
JULY 1ST

As a reflection as I write this in February 2015, last night on television there was a program on BBC2 about some Welsh comedian climbing Kili, with a party of fifty or so others. If nothing else, it brought back more memories of my adventure on the mountain back in 2012. A different route to our climb, a more direct one than tours, going up the east side of Kili, to Gidman's Point then on to the summit. Done slightly later in the year, in September I think it was, there certainly wasn't the snow on the final summit walk that we had on the ground, but it did snow while they did the final summit climb. Unlike us again, the mountain was covered in cloud and fog for them, and on the lower slopes through the rainforest they had a lot of rain; their views of the mountain were few and far between as the fog kept coming down. Happy memories of my climb, though I didn't enjoy their humour on the mountain, I wouldn't have enjoyed such a big party, and missing the views and sights that we saw I think would have been a big disappointment to me. Surprising also how many of them turned back with altitude sickness. A brief aside, but lovely to see "my" mountain again.

We go on, the five of us on our own route.

Little to no sleep again unfortunately, so I spend the hours around dawn clock watching, deciding when I should brave the outside to go to the loo. It feels very cold again. I finally decide at about five fifty in the morning that I shall have to go. So, fighting my way out of the tent again, I find the ground white with a heavy frost. I trip my way around boulders to the loo tent, and it sounds as if someone is following my tracks. The outside temperature being low, means that the simple flushing mechanism of the portaloo has frozen too, so no joy there. Back to the tent across the frosted ground and back into my sleeping bag to keep warm (or try) until it is time to get up. Chris, us old men again, was the other early riser!

As will become the norm over the coming days, I am usually up and dressing or packing when the sound of my early morning drink arrives. I hear him coming so am opening the zips of the tent as he stoops down outside with hot water and the ingredients for our brews. He is learning my habits, so doesn't have to ask, black coffee, two sugars, thank you. Most welcome.

I open the tent doors fully to let in a now truly glorious morning, yes it is cold and the ground all spectacularly white, but in the sunshine, Kili now stands in front of me, a wonderful sight, with the snow fields, the glaciers, all posing in the distance against a brilliant blue sky. A true, good morning. After the arrival of coffee, and tea, we all slowly appear. The arrival (again as will be the norm) of five enamel bowls, with hot water and soap means wash time, and for me, time to shave as well. When this is done, our breakfast is ready so into the mess tent to eat. Everyone seems in good spirits, and unlike me, have slept well, and are ready for the day ahead. The porridge on these cold mornings goes down well, and what we are given certainly does fill us up and set us well for our exertions ahead.

By eight o'clock, we are eaten, dressed and packed ready for the day ahead. As we get to know each other's routines, I am learning it is a great help to the porter in charge of tents, that the earlier we can be out of them, the quicker he can get on with his tasks of dismantling them and getting them packed away for the next part of their journey. So I will try and get all my stuff together and out of the tent by breakfast, so he can get on. This just leaves a small amount of things, e.g. toothbrush, to put away before we set off again. This he appreciates very much, but then, the more we can help each other the better.

Despite the frost, it is warm already, so definitely a shorts and shirt day today, and in the glaring sunshine that we will be walking into, suntan lotion well applied to our exposed extremities, and plenty of water aboard. At eight fifteen, we are ready and set off once again. A gentle stroll, pole, pole on good paths, firstly around the stream, and then on across the Shira Plain, with good views behind of the Shira Ridge and its accompanying hills and peaks. Other groups on the campsite are also stirring and starting to set off, but we are out on our own, heading to an overnight stay at Moir Huts. Other parties will be going on different routes, to Shira 2. They must have packed the camp up quickly this morning because it is not long before the porters with their loads are catching us, passing us and leaving us behind. Jambo.

The paths are good, and the frost is disappearing quickly in this glorious sunshine. The scenery is good with heathers, some shrubs, and as we progress, more and more volcanic boulders, yellowy in colour, and some large ones standing above us. The vegetation is not quite as thick as yesterday, when descending down onto the plain. A few dried up stream beds that when in flow would all eventually join the Ngare Nairobi river before that heads off northwards. And all this time now, we are walking straight towards our mountain, towering in front of us out of the plain. Again, I am surprised how far down the slopes the snow extends.

Stops are easy, a welcome drink in this heat, and a nip behind a boulder when necessary (again more awkward for Claire but she is managing as we are fairly isolated in our solitude).

The path is wider so it is easy to walk side by side. Chris and I get into a long discussion on rugby and England's chances in the home-based 2015 World Cup, their recent tour to South Africa (which of course he had accompanied them to), his insight into the squad, and I should bow to his superior knowledge. All who know me and my rugby, know I am a great Danny Cipriani fan, and though at this time not on the squad's radar for various indiscretions, my opinion has always been that we cannot win the World Cup without him, the X factor he brings when on the field. Everyone has their own opinion, Chris included, but I enjoy a long conversation with him on the subject and think how much Anthony would be enjoying this chat too.

At this stage there is little change in altitude, as we make our way over the plateau, but at least it looks as if Kili is getting closer, despite what will be another four days of walking before the ascent on Uhuru peak and hopefully success. Again, the odd gully of a dried up stream, but this is fairly gentle walking in the heat of the morning sun. Spirits are high as we continue across the plateau, scenery unchanging, getting warmer, so plenty of water stops. It is some time since we have seen another party. In the hot sun, we continue, starting to turn slightly northwards and then starting to ascend gently, it is approaching midday.

We turn a bend to be greeted by our porters, who have set up camp, very basic, with a tent to offer us some shade, water for a wash, and table and chairs for a sit down lunch on the Shira Plateau. They are full of surprises. This is the hottest time of day, and what they have done is fantastic. A yam stew, then fresh oranges, then a drink is served for us and is very refreshing after our morning "stroll".

After a brief rest following lunch, it is time to get underway again, so we load up again and carry on our journey now following round the western slopes of Kili. As seems to happen most days as we will find out, Kili likes an afternoon nap and becomes covered in cloud, so we lose some of our sunshine, and the sky darkens to the north in front of us as it did yesterday. The vegetation markedly thins now as we emerge out of the heathers and moorland, onto more rocky terrain which is harder to walk on, more rugged, and now we have to do some scrambling. It is still warm though.

So with the increasing altitude we are now in another region of the mountain terrain, this classed as Highland Desert. Bare and dull as the sun has now been hidden, Kili to our right and more hills to our left further away, we walk on upwards, now definitely pole, pole. There is a large rocky outcrop in front of us, which has ancient caves in its base, ancient history, but we don't get that close as we bare more towards Kili, passing it on our left. We push closer to the steeper slopes of the mountain on our right, up over a ridge and then start dropping downwards, over another small ridge and there in front of us is our campsite for the night – Moir Hut. A large flat area, surrounded by scree, spreading over towards hills in front of us, where we find our tents being erected, the porters having overtaken us again some time ago. We are camped right on the edge of the site, but behind us are many other tents. It looks a bit like the pictures I have seen of refugee camps. It is two thirty in the afternoon.

Our day has not finished, not yet; we rest for a while, have some tea and then go on an acclimatisation walk, gaining more altitude, before descending back into the camp. Lent Hills are in front of us and a point in the distance, a rocky peak will be our destination, to get used to the thinning air. We do have a short wait while our tents are finished for our use, so we take ourselves back to the top of the ridge we have just descended into the campsite, sit on rocks and rest.

Tea and biscuits, then we prepare to set off at four fifteen for our climb to the rocky outcrops to the west, towering above us.

All we take with us is water and cameras, and another layer of clothing for if necessary. The first part of the walk is flat, taking us across the campsite, past piles of dilapidation, which I presume are old huts fallen into disrepair, endless tents, junk, and similar left around, attributed to our human race, its untidiness and destroyer of all beautiful sites. Kili towers over us to our right, and is starting to re-emerge from his cloud cover, as the sun tries to appear again.

A slow, steady walk as we leave the campsite and start to walk upwards, it is very dusty, with no vegetation at all now. As the clouds cross the sky the temperature varies as to whether the sun is out or not. In this dusty wilderness, we seem to have temporarily exhausted our conversation and continue in silence as the ascent becomes steeper and the scree turns rockier.

We reach the top of the ridge and carry on along the western side of it, hard going now as we come across more and more large boulders that we have to scramble across. In some places we have to pull ourselves up sizeable reaches, and with this we spread out over a longer distance. A couple of the porters have come with us, including Loderick who had joined us the previous day and was our oxygen carrier, carrying a small cylinder and mask equipment with him to administer if one of us got into severe difficulties with the altitude. I had enjoyed a long conversation with him earlier about the similarity in our names, which fascinated him. The scenery has now become just a little monotonous.

How much further will we go? We walk around the two rocky towers that we could see from below, and on reaching the far side of them, we turn back on ourselves, but upwards as we start to climb up the outcrops, to get to their top. There is a lot of scrambling, large strides from rock to rock, while pulling oneself upwards. Taking care where we place our feet, we do eventually reach the top, the top of the Lent Hills, with a flat rock floor to stand on. A large crevice between two large rocks, which we leap across, and then admire the views from our panoramic site.

To the west, towards the setting sun, stretching over the plains and into the distance is Meru again, stretching in solitary magnificence into the sky, the Shira Plateau and Hills, where we have walked over the past day and a half. To the east is Kilimanjaro itself rising above us in the clear blue sky with his snow-covered summit appearing so close from here, but so tall, and it will still be another four days before we will stand on that summit if we can make it that far.

We spend some time chatting on our rocky platform, taking photos of the views, of each other, and of our guides, Chunga, William, Loderick, and Sugar Ray (becoming a firm favourite amongst us for his joy and humour, named by Chris for his likeness to a well-known boxer, he is quite happy to keep his new name). For a couple of them at this lofted elevation, there is some phone reception, so Chris and Neil are able to make a brief telephone call back home to their children.

So admiring the views, we discuss what we have done and what we have to do tomorrow, where we will skirt the lower reaches of the mountain on the Southern Circular path, onwards the next day to take us round to the east side of the mountain, from where we will attempt our summit climb.

As the sun starts to descend in the sky, the air starts getting cooler, and it is time to return to camp. We have done our first altitude acclimatisation, and one of the benefits of this is to go high then return to a lower height while your body adjusts to the lower oxygen content of the air. We have now been up to about 4500 metres and we will return to the camp altitude of 4155 metres. We have to carefully retrace our steps across this rocky terrain, back down and around this rocky tower, before re-joining the dusty path on the volcanic scree. About an hour's walking will get us back near the campsite. It is exceptionally dusty as we get near to the camp again in the fast-fading sunlight. The sunset is interesting, some colours, but gets hidden behind our westerly ridge. We have done this descent at our own pace, so become spread out a bit, but as we reach Moir Hut again, we find that Neil is the first to be feeling the effects of altitude sickness.

Altitude sickness, or acute mountain sickness is the main fear in terms of health that people have when attempting this climb; it can be a serious condition and it can affect anyone. By being aware of the symptoms, one can get the condition yet get through it by observing the rules of acclimatisation, hence our extra walk today. As one gets higher, the air gets thinner, pressure drops and less oxygen is available in the atmosphere. This is noticeable above 2500m. High altitude is classed as above 3700m and very high altitude above 5500m. Above this is extreme altitude and heart and lungs have to work very hard to oxygenate the body, making blood become less efficient at acquiring and transporting oxygen. A slow, gradual ascent will allow the body to adjust, but the time of this adjustment will vary from person to person. Early signs are fatigue, headache (as if you have a hangover) and loss of appetite. Carefully managing your ascent here will probably get you through it, and this is the condition which Chunga mentioned at the start that his word was final in our continued climb. If he thought we were not adjusting, then we would be sent back down the mountain. If the condition deteriorates, the headache becomes more severe, you become lethargic, confused, disorientated, with severe breathing difficulties following. Ataxia may follow, and this is when pulmonary or cerebral oedema may be setting in, which can result in unconsciousness and even death within twelve hours. The brain will swell and cease to function properly. So, it is very serious, and Neil is the first victim amongst us.

A quick wash as our supper is ready on our return to the campsite, so we head to the tent to eat, with little natural light left. By now, Neil is suffering, so doesn't join us, preferring to take himself off to his sleeping bag and rest. Tonight, carrot soup, followed by spaghetti bolognese, a vegetable stir fry, and then fruit. We really are being spoilt in our cuisine, and if I thought I would lose weight on this trip, it isn't going to happen. We eat very well, chat as usual, and obviously there is some concern about Neil. We retire to our tents; it is cold but not as cold as last night, and again I, after getting my bed ready, try to sleep, again unsuccessfully.

An interesting day, getting to know the others better, we are becoming more and more of a unit. It was very hot up to lunchtime, then dull to the camp and then we saw the sun again for our acclimatisation walk, which other than some hard rock scrambling, I feel okay after. I'm fine at the moment, as I lie under the shadow of Kilimanjaro. Moir Hut to me is not the most attractive place in the world, ramshackle and untidy, but we will be moving on tomorrow, away from this place. The amount of litter and trash that is left around the mountain is a real shame, especially as this is the country's main tourist attraction, and unless anything is done about it, it will only get worse. But then, as visitors we also have a duty to look after their treasure which they are giving us brief use of.

We are making progress, and we are enjoying each other's company. The porters are friendly, and helpful and want us to enjoy our trek, and succeed.

I really do hope Neil does feel better in the morning after a good night's sleep, he certainly did look rough before he retired to bed. And, I hope the rest of us are okay too.

12. MOIR HUTS TO LAVA TOWER
JULY 2ND 2012

Today we are allowed a lie in, until seven o'clock, especially with Neil suffering the night before, but as is becoming the norm, and is now beginning to concern me, my sleep was very poor, with the cold and the hard mountain floor I can't settle and other than dozing a little, that is it. So I rise at about six. Sitting up suddenly, I find my head spinning, and there is no way that I can say that I feel 100%. My stomach also feels that it has had better days – is the start of altitude sickness for me, or am I starting a tummy thing?

I rise and start packing again, sometimes having to stop just to re-orientate myself, doing this until my morning coffee arrives, and it is time to wash and shave. The familiar morning routine. At the moment it is overcast with Kili shrouded in low cloud. I don't feel well, no Neil, and Chris and Jeff don't feel 100% either. Breakfast is taken but I don't feel that hungry now, so I eat a little, drink plenty, and then it is time to get ready to begin today's walk ahead of us.

We finish packing and are ready to set off at 8.15 a.m., taking it very slowly to begin with for Neil's sake, who certainly is suffering, and me also. I feel some dejection, worrying that this is this going to be the end of my journey, with stomach cramps, headache and dizziness. Our route takes us uphill back out of the campsite the way we had come yesterday, Kili's slopes on our left and from here, Meru to our right in the distance. After an initial climb, with the sun now out and the summit in full view, the path levels off as we continue to walk in this moorland/desert landscape. Dry, arid dust, some large heathers but the vegetation is diminishing.

To help Neil, his luggage (rucksack and water bottles) are being carried for him, and he doesn't look well, grey complexion and looking very strained. We try and chat with him but it is a struggle for him. Me, I still hurt but grit my teeth and push myself on, but am well aware now that I am suffering badly and not improving, is this the end of the road?

The scenery is now very similar to that we experienced yesterday when walking from Shira Camp, but despite all the other tents at Moir Hut, we have our solitude again as if we were the only people on the mountain. I recall a friend at Christmas telling me how he had hated every step as all he saw was lines of people walking, zig zagging across the mountain and how fed up he became being one of them, a monotony to him. This came back into my mind now as all seemed so empty. We start to head southwards as we follow the Southern Circular Path around the mountain, and we can see Lava Tower away in the distance, our destination for tonight.

And then as the plateau extends away to our right, again I reflect on what Kevin had said about the "crowds" as in the distance we begin to see more and more people coming towards us, porters walking quickly, the trekkers less so. This is where there will be a convergence of routes, where the Lemosho and the more popular Machame routes join. We stop for a break, and it is as if we are about to join the M25 walking route up Kilimanjaro. Lots of "Jambo," as porters pass us.

The vegetation is now sparse, dusty yellow volcanic desert, with some large outcrops of laval rock and scree surrounding the path. We are on the move again, joining, overtaking other groups but making way for the hard-working porters as they pass with their burdens on their heads. The path undulates, and then there is a high cliff face on our left. To show the difference in the fee-paying trekkers and the locals, we come across a single Japanese man, smartly dressed in "jungle" attire, with parasol, and walking behind him is a porter carrying a bed on his head for him. Creature comforts on the mountain, but then if I had this perhaps I would sleep, I wish!! I wonder what the porters think of this, two worlds collide.

After half an hour, we leave the main route, and head northwards towards the mountain, and the large black rock which is Lava Tower, standing out from the rest of the terrain. This is now an uphill climb, quite steep but it is relatively easy walking even in the full sun. We are on our own again now as we climb, everyone else heading towards Barranco. As we near the top of the ridge, between the steep slopes of Kili (we are near to these now) and Lava Tower, we can see wooden huts in front of us, our next campsite, the drop down toilets at Lava Camp. As we go over the ridge we drop down into a deserted campsite bar our own tents. The camp is quite flat for a change so we are well spread out, but as usual our good porters have erected the site before our arrival, and are busy cooking our lunch.

Our tents ready, we have time to get our bedding etc. out, unpack a little and relax for a while. Our tents are basically two-man tents, quite quick to erect, with fitted ground sheet and two layers, the tent and an outer fitted wind sheet, with the two sets of zips that I so struggled with in the night on the early part of the trip. Comfortable but not high enough to stand in, and one tries not to bring in too much dust and grit as we crawl in.

Lunch is ready, so the familiar wash with hot water, and then to eat. Zucchini soup, followed by chicken and chips. That has given Neil his appetite back, the best meal we have had so far, I am very impressed with this cooking. This is a nice campsite as well in the shadows of Kili and Lava Rock, and the slopes going up to the Western Breach, and behind us Meru is following us in our tracks. Glorious sunshine, desolate other than one other small party which has camped near the Tower, we are just accompanied by a few gigantic ravens, searching the site for food. Lunch was good and now we can rest and relax before we will once again do an acclimatisation walk up the slopes towards the Western Breach, and the Arrow Glacier, which we will start at three. Neil will decide how he feels but probably has to do it to be able to carry on, me, I do feel a lot better than I did, so am pleased to be able to relax for an hour or so in this peaceful spot, reading and feeling better in myself. A gentle stroll towards the huts and the Tower, this is relaxing and probably what I need.

At three we set off again, Neil coming with us but again has his bag carried for him. It is sunny and cloudless as we walk up a gentle gradient towards the mountain face in front of us. For the first time, I decide it is time I start getting used to my walking poles, as I would be starting to use them in the next couple of days and thought I would have to get used to them. We cross the odd trickle of a mountain stream descending from higher slopes, where the snow line actually doesn't seem that far away now. In the distance, high above us in the snow, we catch a glimpse of two climbers descending the slope through the snow. Bare rocks, some boulders, easy walking to begin with but as usual pole, pole because this is the highest we have been and we are going higher.

Chunga tries to correct the way I use the poles, but I seem to have adapted my own style which I am happy with, using shorter poles than the others. We then start to ascend the slope, steeper now with the harder rock underfoot changing to rocky scree. However, I feel good and am quite happy again, willing to take the lead with William. More steeply we go, crossing stream beds with icy surrounds where our footing has to be very careful, shaded from the sun by rocks so never seeing sunlight. We do seem in good spirits, and despite reaching heights not yet achieved, we are all coping fine. Who knows how far up we are going but the legs are working well and I'm not worried now like I was this morning. Neil jokes about having his equipment carried for him, and seems better in himself now. I am having to frequently adjust my stride pattern as the nature of my footings changes, but am finding it relatively easy, and we are at this time only about a Scafell away from the summit, even if we are a couple of days away yet. This has made me feel a lot more confident again.

Upwards we continue, our only other company a few of these noisy crows, and in the distance in the snow we admire one of their nests, with the fledglings raising their heads above the parapets in the rocks. Scrambling on up, we eventually reach a point where we will go no higher today, the highest I have ever been and an altitude I will only reach again on the final summit walk, some 4800 metres above sea level.

We take in our surrounds, taking a drink as well (sippy sippy), before starting our descent back down to our camp at Lava Tower. We are starting to lose the sun as it descends to the west, and with this the temperature starts to fall noticeably as well. We make our way down, Sugar Ray with us who again we have a good laugh with; he and Chris have struck up a funny relationship full of humour. I am getting used to the poles now, and will use them from here onwards, they are certainly a great help going down, using them for a steadying guide to help my feet. The descent is not hard but as the evening draws in and we make our way down, it is getting cooler and cooler. We are pleased Neil feels better, and we are as one again as we approach the campsite.

Back to flatter ground, and then back into camp, an acclimatisation walk successfully completed and quite refreshing. A wash and get ready for supper which the cooks have prepared for us while we were out. A welcome drink of coffee also awaits our return.

It's about six o'clock now and as we wait for supper, I take myself off towards Meru and the huts where we had entered the camp earlier. The sun is now setting in the west, behind Meru, and I am about to witness the most amazing sunset I have ever seen. A pity the others are not with me to see this, as I stand in awe at what is in front of me the most dazzling oranges, reds and yellows, such deep colours to the right of Meru. Is this what I had come to see on my mountain quest? Oh what fantastic sights Africa has to offer. I take a couple of photos on my phone camera (which came out surprisingly well for the distance involved but doesn't do full justice to what is in front of me), before with the ever-changing light, the sun disappears behind the distant hills and is gone.

Sheer beauty for a few moments, and something to remember forever, not to be seen again while on the mountain, though I was hopeful every night. What an amazing thing nature is.

I wander slowly back to the dinner tent, tearing myself away from what I have just seen. Last into the tent, I can only tell the others what I have seen, and what they have missed, then show them what I have recorded on camera.

Supper arrives, bean soup followed by chilli con carne, but we are all tired now, struggling tonight and with appetites that are small. A lot of the meal is unfinished, though it was very good. The chef comes to see us, to ask if the cooking is not good enough, and we assure him his efforts are brilliant, but there is just far too much for us, we are sorry and just can't do it justice today, but we are really grateful for his efforts.

Chunga tells us about tomorrow, when we will head away from the summit, skirting round the southern slopes, so we can approach the summit climb from the south east/eastern route, and a long day of walking in front of us. With that and the rapidly falling temperature at the highest we have camped so far, it is time to return to our tents and time to snuggle down into our sleeping bags for warmth and I hope, sleep. Oh for that bed I had seen earlier.

For me, I can reflect back on that wonderful sunset. A good day in the end which started with despair as to whether I was going to suffer from altitude sickness, but varied and spectacular in the end. In days, we are halfway through the trip, in altitude, the summit has been tangibly close, the scenery varied and interesting.

For now, we have bonded well, but will now drop height as we get into a position to go for the summit.

On we go tomorrow.

13. THE BARRANCO VALLEY
JULY 3RD 2012

We are due for an early start today again, rising at about six o'clock, but ten minutes before this, I am up and about after another sleepless and uncomfortable night. I sit up in my sleeping bag and *bang*, my head is spinning again, just like yesterday morning. This will be a bad day again.

Coffee arrives and the usual morning ritual begins, washing, packing, and getting ready for the walk ahead. The sun is not up yet so there is still a chill in the air, very cold in fact. We are due to set off today at 7.15, so there is no great rush at the moment, and again I have my habit of packing most of my bedding etc. before breakfast while having my coffee. Breakfast time arrives and to be honest, I don't feel that good, dizzy and not that hungry. I do eat a little but more in the knowledge of a long day's walking ahead rather than actually being hungry. Neil still feels a little under the weather, but better than he was, the others are fine. So breakfast finishes and we finish our packing in preparation for a prompt start at the appointed time. This will be our longest walk other than the summit climb, and we will actually lose quite a lot of altitude over the course of the day, over undulating terrain.

It would later transpire that despite feeling grotty, this would turn out to be a varied and exhilarating day's walking as we continue on the Southern Circular path onto Karanga. Unfortunately my recollection of the earlier part of the walk is sketchy due to my head, but I can say this is where I really missed my camera.

So as we muster together under Lava Tower, well wrapped

up and with gloves on for the first time, as it is bitterly cold in the shade with the wind blowing, our first steps take us gently upwards, skirting the tower; easy walking, little vegetation and not rocky. We head away from the mountain and the southern steep slopes.

Passing a signpost, which looks quite odd in the middle of nowhere, pointing in all directions – Lava Tower, Arrow Glacier, Barranco – we go over the top of a ridge and then as the sun starts to appear, out of the shadow of Kilimanjaro, we begin to descend gently. Thank heavens it is getting warmer. This is at about 4530 metres, and in the ever-increasing sunshine, from here we start to drop quite quickly through a series of zigzags into a gully. The scenery starts to change quite dramatically now as we leave the alpine desert scenery of yesterday and return to moorland, and we start to see an array of plants we have not encountered yet. *Senecio kilimanjari*, some towering up to 5 metres high, have tall stems that collect and store water, the stems supporting large cabbage-like clumps of leaves. They apparently flower about once every twenty-five years, before branching, then a quarter of a century later, repeating the process. Its growing shoot is protected by a dense leaf bud that insulates it, and when it does flower, it produces long mustard or yellow (depending on the Senecio species) coloured flowers, forming spikes. Then there are the endemic moorland Lobelias, standing up to 3 metres tall, with a hollow stem and a pronounced flower spike that supports spiralling leaf-like bracts that hide small blue flowers. They are also designed to protect their growing bud from sub-zero temperatures with a rosette of leaves surrounding it. Other grasses, thistles, and shrubs line rocky ridges, and we do see occasional bird life.

We plunge down into the Barranco Valley, spectacular and formed from a huge landslide that swept southwards down from the summit some 100,000 years ago. The valley in places is some 300 metres deep. I wish that I could really appreciate this beauty and that I could picture it for posterity, but oh my head hurts. Claire takes many pictures, and bless her heart she keeps coming and checking on both Neil and I, concerned because she knows we are suffering. We wind our way towards Barranco Camp which we can see in the distance in front of us, zigzagging up and down and across ridges as we make our way down the valley, surrounded by this new vegetation we have come across. A stream runs by the side of us in places, sometimes us having to cross it, and now and again the most stunning waterfall, and anyone who knows me, knows I like my waterfalls. I reluctantly don't use my phone camera very much as I don't want to run the battery down for the summit and one or two messages to say I'm okay, and if I had succeeded or not.

For two hours we walk down this spectacular valley in our solitude, spectacular scenery, beautiful scenery, talking as we go, though today often about what is in front of us. We stop from time to time for water and snack breaks as it is now getting very hot. The camp in the distance looks very upmarket compared to what we have seen, huts, decent-looking loos from a distance, and a flat area in front where if available, a helicopter could land if there was an emergency on the mountain. We had already come across the Kili ambulance, what one might describe as a metal bed on two wheels with a pulling handle, it certainly didn't look very comfortable. But with altitude sickness this could be lifesaving in extreme cases. From the campsite, other parties are leaving and heading towards a conjoining path that we shall meet shortly.

As we reach the bottom of the valley, wandering towards the camp, we reach a junction of paths where we are directed east to our next part of the trail. We can see the spectacular views of the southern face of Kibo, the Western Breach, and the Heim Glacier, with its moraine crumbling down towards the campsite. But in front of us, and it said nothing about this in the brochure, is the Barranco Wall, a 300 metre climb up what looks like a nearly sheer cliff as we stand at the bottom, but above us there is a steady stream of climbers and porters making their way up, the porters of course carrying their normal loads. So surely we can manage it.

We cross the stream, quite deep in places, and take a short break before we tackle our ascent. Claire again checks that I'm okay, offering me encouragement as we set off. Jeff is in the lead behind William, then Neil who still has his bag carried for him, followed by Chris, Claire, with me at the rear, and of course Chunga who is observing and checking on all of us as we proceed.

It is a well-defined path, winding its way up the wall, bare earth amongst the groundsel-covered face of the wall. No use for poles here so they are stashed away in my rucksack. Steep gradients using your hands to hang on to the wall face, and places where you have to pull yourself up with your arms, reaching across ledges, make it a long, slow haul up the Barranco Wall. At times, we have to pull ourselves into the side to let more nimble porters pass us by, then on and on, up we go. The occasional stop for breath and a drink, then pull ourselves on up (this is a bit reminiscent of the later parts of my climb up Snowden with Jenny), some false dawns as we think we are there but find a further rising around the next bend. Claire takes a few pictures as I climb below her, and sometimes it feels as if I am hanging over backwards, with the (light) weight of my rucksack, as I scramble round a ledge. It is hot, the sun full out now.

As this happens, I start to get a degree of neck pain, and this is contributing to my discomfort, a recurrence of previous whiplash injuries, exacerbated by the lack of sleep and discomfort lying in the tent at night, putting a strain on my neck. With this, and despite the effort of this section of the walk/climb, I start to do some of the neck exercises I had been taught in physiotherapy, which slowly but surely is helping; the headache is going and I start to feel a lot better.

After some hour and a bit, we at last reach the top of the

Wall, quite a climb and view as we look down at where we have just been, back down into the valley. The path winds itself along to a rocky outcrop, a large bare rock where we will stop for lunch. Other parties have stopped here too, a place to view our surrounds from on high in the heat of the day. This will be the last of our packed lunches, thank goodness, I haven't enjoyed any of them. Chicken okay, but the rest! Have to keep the calories up though, especially after the exertion we have just experienced. But this is the food they have, so be thankful, it would be a luxury for those back in the native villages.

It is nice to relax in the sunshine. Claire has been wonderfully supportive today so far to both Neil and I with our difficulties, especially since Chunga has been monitoring us closely as we get closer and closer to the final push.

Lunch is over and we continue on our way with a gentle descent into the next gulley, again using the walking poles now. Perhaps there was a degree of altitude sickness affecting me, and I was the only one taking medication for it, but whether it has been our descent to lower levels, or the neck exercises, or both, I do now feel fine again. Neil also seems a little better now.

Having crossed another little stream in this gully, we now start to walk along a flattish gravel area, unfortunately littered with toilet paper and other rubbish (what a pity people don't respect the mountain more!). Strangely, for all the people at the top of the wall, we seem to be on our own again as we pass through a series of small valleys before crossing a very barren landscape. Not hard walking but still pole, pole as William leads us, now in silence further eastwards. It still seems strange that in just over twenty-four hours now we will be attempting our summit walk, as we walk parallel to the southern slopes and glaciers of Kibo, above us to the north.

There is another change of scenery as we enter the edge of the Karanga valley and we start to descend down the lusher, western slopes, quite steep and covered in heathers, ferns, and other low vegetation. Our descent follows a stream, so is wet underfoot, and in the shade frozen so we have to place our feet carefully, and my pole technique I find a great help in getting down, winding across the stream. We see some icicles, and in places lichen on the rocks. For a little guy like me, some of the steps down are quite challenging, long strides down onto slippery surfaces, sometimes turning to help those behind me down as well. Slow but surefooted, it would be calamitous if one were to slip and fall here.

Spectacular walking, tough, but again more interesting with greenery and some birdlife. Isolated but beautiful in its solitude, testing our abilities with our different physical make-ups, but on we go until we reach the bottom. We emerge out of the shadow of the surrounding rocks back into sunshine, and walk on between taller shrubs, seeing a stream tumbling down from the glaciers above, before as the land becomes flatter, starting to meander through the valley floor. Large boulders, Lobelias and Senecio stand around us as we cross the valley floor until we reach a larger stream. This is like a green oasis on the mountainside – the stream, birds, and flowers are a wonderful sight.

This is however, the last place we can get water before the summit, and we meet porters here filling up the plastic drums before carting it back up to the next campsite, now not far away. What they collect here they will carry to the next two campsites, so now we will have to be frugal with what we use. Chunga says they will come back here if necessary to refill, but we cannot ask them to do that if we are too extravagant with our usage. We also fill all our bottles, and can sterilise the water when we arrive at Karanga campsite.

It is a wonderfully peaceful spot, but now on to our next campsite, the Karanga Valley campsite. Although strictly speaking, we will be out of the valley. On continuing our walk we are faced with the other side of the valley. Another steep path zigzagging up the face of the valley, about a twenty,

twenty-five minute haul up the slope, again myself happy to tag along at the back, beginning to feel a little tired after our day's exertions, but pleased the end is in sight. Unlike descending down into the valley, this is dry and dusty with the full sunshine on our backs, but the steps and pull ups are not so long, so although it is energetic, it is not so physically draining as going up the Barranco Wall.

Strangely enough, it now seems very crowded again as we are joined by others climbing out of the valley, with a procession of porters on water duty. As always, it seems the top is just over the next ridge, but for once it is and to our right along the top of the valley wall is our campsite. We are set up at the far end of this ramshackle site amongst boulders, perched on the edge of the wall, with magnificent views over to Meru, sticking out above the clouds, and a vast white woolly panorama stretching out to the south. Somewhere down there is Africa. It is 2.15 in the afternoon, hot in this exposed campsite, but I would imagine in harsher weather it would be hell just here. We are indeed lucky.

Our tents as usual are ready and after a brief organise of the inside, we wash, though here sharing bowls to conserve that precious water. A cup of tea, and then a chance to rest. Even at this altitude you can strip to the waist to wash and still not feel a chill.

We all retire to our tents to get some rest, sleep if possible, and I try using my Puffa as a mattress to soften my bed. Sleep if possible as tomorrow will be a long day; I read a little and then close my eyes for a bit if only to relax.

Tea time, and now the campsite is considerably busier, but in our little corner we are not disturbed and so it remains relatively peaceful. No-one can grab our space. The sun is starting to go down, and with it the air temperature starts to fall so we put on some warmer clothing to keep warm. No spectacular sunset tonight (but at least I got to see one). We will eat with Chunga as usual, and then William will join us to go through the next forty-eight hours – a briefing for the summit walk.

Tonight we have pumpkin soup, followed by a frankfurter concoction, then fruit as the norm, as by now we have realised that Chunga has a bit of a penchant for fruit, and we tease him as he eats more and more that we place in front of him. An enjoyable meal, following the rigours of our walk today.

We laugh and joke over a hot drink, before William joins us, and he and Chunga talk us through tomorrow night. Clothing, water, and the weather are discussed as we are told of the plan for the day. We start with a short walk to Barafu Hut – base camp for the summit strike – and then a relaxing day, check in at the registration hut, then an early night, getting up at about eleven to eat and be on the move by midnight.

The early weather forecast is of it staying clear; no snow is forecast, temperatures with wind-chill going down to about -11°C. William, Chunga, and three porters will accompany us. All being well, we will reach the roof of Africa at sunrise, about seven in the morning, and then the descent back down to the campsite. William gives a long talk about the walk, and all it involves, on what will be a long, tiring day. But this is what we have come for, so it is now or never, so close but so far.

We ask a few questions; Chris and Jeff are both concerned about the amount of clothing they may have to wear and worried they will be too hot inside the many layers. We prepare ourselves, support each other and offer encouragement. Neil and Jeff are in competitive spirit about who will summit first, the rest of us will be pleased to stand at Uhuru Peak when we get there. WE will do it as one.

We retire to the tents to rest. I think the adrenaline is now starting to pump; Kili towers above us in the moonlight, within touching distance, another forty-eight hours and we hopefully will have summited and be halfway down again. The fulfilment of a lifetime ambition is so close now.

Bed.

And time to reflect on a wonderful day, in hindsight starting to feel really rough, but as the day progressed, fantastic walking. What amazing scenery in both the Barranco and Karanga valleys. The vegetation, birdlife, and all along towering above us, about to welcome us (or not) was Kilimanjaro, his peak, ice fields, and glaciers way above us as we skirted around his circular path. I really wish today I had had my camera. But for all our walking today and climbing high walls, we were actually a lot lower than we started. Lava, 4640, and now at Karanga, a mere 4035 metres.

There is lot to think about as I settle down to sleep, relatively comfortably. I am warm (although it has taken a while to sort that side of it out), and tired. Sleep may or may not come, but for sure, I am a little apprehensive now. I know that Kilimanjaro will await us tomorrow, but I am going to succeed, I know I am, determination or the Wood stubbornness will see me stand on top.

Sweet dreams – I wish.

Sunset over Meru, from Lava Camp.

The snows get closer, alpine desert with the Western Breach behind.

The Barranco Valley with its amazing flora.

Jeff and Neil on the Barranco Wall, where did it say about this in the brochure!

Above the clouds, me at Karanga, Meru behind me.

The slopes to the Western Breach.

Camping in the sky. Our three tents at Karanga.

Barafu Hut and our ascent route to the summit when it gets dark.

14. NEARLY – BUT NOT QUITE
JULY 4TH 2012

Karanga to Barafu Hut. 4035-4640 metres.

An easy day today, in preparation for the big one tomorrow. Perched on our rock edge, high over the African plains, hidden by cloud, and with only Meru and Kilimanjaro above us, they are all that we can see.

The previous night we had negotiated a lie-in of sorts, rising at seven, as long as we were on the road by eight thirty, instead of the suggested time of six to get up. Though not as high as Lava Tower, at this altitude it was not a warm night, and sleep had been for me non-existent, but after days of practice, there was at least a modicum of comfort. And best of all this morning, no headache, I feel fine.

I have read so many reports of this camp, covered in cloud and rain, but as I rise and open my tent to that welcoming cup of coffee, I get up to a gorgeous morning, cloudless blue sky with the summit, with his snow-covered slopes rising to the glaciers nearby, standing out distinctly. The cloud below us makes it seem like we are floating on air. If this is a bleak sight – and I would imagine very bare, bleak and unwelcoming if the weather were against us – our vista this morning certainly gives an impetus to what we are trying to achieve.

The usual ritual of washing, last shave for a while, us tough guys standing bare-chested in the morning sun, not cold in her rays. Packing again so my tent will be vacated by breakfast so my dear tent man can get to work dismantling it, when the breakfast call arrives I am virtually done and ready for the off.

A good breakfast started off with porridge – we will eat a lot today, to build up our calories for our "night stroll". Without much effort we are easily ready by eight thirty, as a lot of other parties are also getting ready to begin their walk, the relatively short hike to Barafu.

We are underway, and a definite pole, pole now as we will ascend some 600 metres today to reach the next camp, but we have no need to rush and risk altitude problems as we are so close now. We all seem fine this morning and so are as one again. Neil is back to his normal self again, joking as he walks along. The scenery is basically just volcanic scree, yellow dust with the odd large or group of boulders standing high above. This is a very gentle ascent, with many groups now on the march. We intermingle, pass other groups on what is a very casual walk, some being Brits, some other nationalities.

We come across a group of South Africans, mainly women, and to our amusement Casanova Chunga thinks he will try chatting them up. Three ladies together, he tries his luck with just general chit chat, much to our amusement as we walk just behind him, light-hearted and entertaining as we walk alongside their party for a while. And then he blows it; how nice it is to see three generations of women all tackling the mountain together, daughter, mother, and grandmother. Oops. If one did look more mature than the others, they are actually college friends. Chunga, much to our amusement with his failure, retreats behind us all to cover his embarrassment. We talk with them for a few minutes, wish them well on their summit attempt, and then move on ahead of them.

In full sunlight it is warm work, and only in light clothing, we take care with our water provisions as we don't want to send our porters back down into the Karanga Valley. Calls of nature are governed by the availability of the nearest rock, and all this time Kibo looms as we look to our left. The landscape is unchanging, a gentle gradient up, volcanic dust on this alpine desert; vegetation is a rarity, with a rocky ridge directly in front of us getting closer and closer. Our three-hour walk will end when we climb this up to the camp at Barafu Hut.

The gentle walk is abruptly ended as we reach the ridge, in essence the start of the final climb to the summit, as it will now be all rock until we reach the snow-covered brim of the crater above. A gentle walk so far, perhaps we are now going to do most of the 600 metres we have to do today. This really is a scramble up rocky paths, up to the top of this ridge from where we turn westwards towards the mountain top. A well-worn path takes us up towards Barufu Hut, holding camp for the final challenge at midnight. A short climb and we are in the campsite, a sprawling mass of tents wherever there may be a space between rocks. We wind our way between tents until we reach the spot where our trusty porters have already pitched our camp, mess tent by the side of the path and our tents just below, where rocks allow, and the loo tent under the ridge above us. For the first time we seem very cramped, especially with the constant stream of people filing past us to look for a spare bit of ground themselves.

We have a lot of time to kill now, time to relax, rest, think about what to wear and take on the final assault, to basically prepare for the ascent.

They will try and load us with food – carbs – for the night ahead, for the long journey we are about to begin. A hot drink on arrival, it is only coffee time in fact after our short walk this morning, then we unpack, chatting amongst ourselves, offering help if needed, unpacking and starting to get ourselves prepared for our night hike. We are in touching distance, but it is getting so crowded now in this campsite, as other groups come in trying to find a space to pitch a tent. And by now there is a trickle of people who have succeeded today, and are about to start their descent.

Mid-afternoon in this sunny position on the side of the mountain, and we have to wind our way further up the slope, avoiding others tents and guy ropes, as Chunga takes us to the new hut, built on the side of the ridge, where we have to register our arrival at the camp and climb date. It is very warm even at this altitude. We each in turn fill in the normal forms, name, passport number etc., and while doing this, a Japanese party enter the hut, having just come down from the summit, and some of them look near exhaustion (we should, all being well, be down earlier than this before the real heat of the day). They are looking for aid, but there is little we can do to help; they must find their base and get assistance, probably water and a rest will help.

Having all registered, we amble down back to our tents, taking the time to view the panorama seen from the top of the ridge. Below us on the other side, even more tents appear as people arrive from the shorter Rongai route, and across the alpine desert, the third of these standalone volcanoes, Mawenzi, standing at 4535 metres (Meru and Kili being the others). It is a spectacular sight in the brilliant sunlight, set against a blue sky background. Apparently now forbidden to climb due to the crumbly nature of the volcanic rock faces, it still offers a wonderful sight standing out alone in the desert.

The whole place is busy, with people preparing for the ascent as the clock ticks away – only a few hours now before departure. It will be -11°C with wind-chill, but with only light winds predicted, it could be a lot worse. Clothing, I will wear seven layers on top, three layers over my legs, and feet, well, I don't know – here is a balance between warmth and comfort. One of the last things I had bought before leaving were some little ankle socks that would breathe, very thin, to fit inside my walking socks. I try these on now, walking socks and then boots, and try a brief stroll. My feet will no doubt swell when walking, and no, this is not comfortable, so foot attire will be the same as the rest of the walk up, though I will use a clean pair of socks and hope that is enough to keep them warm. Other items of clothing are probably a bit smelly now after their constant use over the past few days, but changes of clothes would be an unnecessary luxury to drag up the mountain.

Two vests, a rugby shirt, body warmer, fleece, down jacket and waterproof/windproof coat. Long johns, walking trousers and then windproof/waterproof overtrousers. Jeff and Chris were still arguing over this but were eventually allowed to part with one of these layers; they are better covered than me. Double gloves, hat, scarf and walking poles – and keeping as little as possible in our rucksack, to lighten our load.

We have a briefing over an early supper, William and Chunga telling us about the conditions, the type of climb, the other people up there and the importance of pole, pole. It will be a hard climb in freezing conditions. We should keep our water bottles inside our down coats to keep them from freezing and carry them upside down – water freezes from the top, so if that does happen, the nozzles at the bottom will still be ice free. The use of torches and conserving batteries, and safety issues; with the five of us will go five of them, Chunga, William, Sugar Ray, Loderick, and one other whose name sadly I cannot remember.

Chunga offers to check clothing, and it is here Chris and Jeff finally win their argument, he checks mine and I am worried that I will be too warm but we agree I will wear as stipulated, better to be too hot than too cold, especially if the weather were to suddenly turn against us.

All preparations are completed, we have travelled seven days to be here, now so near but so far. They estimate we will summit at about eight o'clock, around sunrise, eight hours' hard continuous walking with little oxygen. And then we have to come down, descend to the next camp way below us. It will be a long, hard day, are we ready for it? All will be revealed in but a few hours now.

Now it is time to get some rest as best we can and then it will be time to go. I haven't slept on the mountain yet and I don't think now will be any different.

We have done all that we can do and but now wait to see what tomorrow brings – BUT – I know now that I am going to succeed, to fulfil that lifetime ambition.

15. THE FINAL PUSH
JULY 5TH 2012

And so, this is it. Strictly it is still the 4th, but our day is about to begin. Barafu Hut to Uhuru Peak, 4640 metres up to 5895 metres, the top of Kilimanjaro, the "Roof of Africa". If I am to ramble over the next few pages, I won't apologise as this is what I have set out to achieve, the fulfilment of a lifetime dream, and this will mean so much to me, if – when – I achieve my goal. And, let's not forget, we have to come down. This will be a hard day, potentially the hardest day of my little life, but if it turns out the way I hope, wow, it will stay with me forever.

It's just before eleven o'clock now, and to say I was rested would be an exaggeration, having lain restlessly in my sleeping bag for the past few hours, not that comfortable. I don't know if it was for the purposes of the climb, but last night's supper, was to say the least rather salty, and had left that horrible dry throat and stuffiness in your head, but we had to eat to take in the necessary calories. It is time to rise, and it is now or never. So I, along with a good number of others, am now rising, trying to conserve battery power, so uncomfortably trying to dress in the dark, with all these layers to put on as well. Not being a wearer of long johns before, this was a real trial trying to put my legs in these. So layer went on top of layer, but before we go too far with this we had better attend to the natural duties of the body before becoming too ensconced in clothing. As usual the night temperature is cold, and it will only get colder as we climb, as said before, possibly down to -11°C. The shirts, fleeces, everything made ready earlier in the evening, are now on. A few things in my rucksack, phone, water, biscuits, Kendal Mint Cake (well-travelled and still I haven't touched it) and it is off to the mess tent to meet up with the others for a warm drink and some very warming porridge. Our mood, good but subdued in the half light of the tent, Chris and Jeff still going on about the worry of overheating in three layers of leggings, but they have won their argument and will wear what they wish to. I would have to admit that I do feel like the Michelin man in all these layers, and a call of nature could be interesting (and painful if Jack Frost were to nip in uninvited!!).

Suitably fed, and warmed by the hot drink and porridge inside us, it is time for final preparations; gaiters on, a couple of water bottles secreted upside down inside my Puffa, the two sets of gloves on over each other, and finally Dave's waterproof to be my outer layer. A woolly hat covers my ears, my scarf round my neck, and covering high up over my face. I am ready. Not quite, torch fitted over my hat, rucksack on my back, and hands through the loops on my walking poles. Lastly, a final adjustment of my bootlaces so they are not too tight, and I close up the tent. Messy boy, no tidying now. We will do it when we come down again later! We congregate outside the mess tent.

There is much activity around this vast campsite as other parties are readying themselves for their walk, and already we start to see a small procession of torch lights ascending up the path out of the camp towards our destiny.

It is nearly midnight and now it is time to do what we came to do. The ten of us about to leave, five of us walkers and the five porters including William and Chunga, one each in case one of us drops out – there will always be enough to accompany the unlucky person down, but enough to accompany us on our ascent. All our other porters have come out to wish us well and good luck, *Kwa heri*, goodbye. *Asante*, we thank them, then we are on our way, the summit eight to nine hours ahead of us.

Pole, pole for what seems forever, we wind our way out of the camp, zigzagging through and around other camping parties, quietly and in single file. Some tents are still quiet, some show the beginnings of activity for those who in the near future will be following our footsteps. We pass the registration hut we visited yesterday afternoon and eventually out of the city of tents.

The path, having left the huts, starts to steepen upwards, and a steady pace is adopted that at this time doesn't seem too tiring in my overdressed body. Single file we go, taking an early look up the slope, of which in the course of the night there will be many, the steady torchlight trail winds its way on ahead of us. We do have the light of a full moon to help us a bit, but as we start to scramble up our rocky path, soon catching our breath, I can't say that this stage is the most memorable, the sight of me putting one foot in front of the other on the loose rock we walk over. The cold hits my face; my hands and feet are okay at the moment, and at the moment conversation is limited. Frequent glances upwards, it's not getting any closer.

We have the occasional stop for water, only brief stops as I struggle to delve into my layers of clothing to find the upturned bottles secreted within, and then clumsily trying to do the zips up again with the double layer of gloves on. Sometimes Chunga would help me or one of the others achieve this simple task.

It is hard to know what we are walking on, frozen scree or rock, but it is hard underfoot, so firm placement of the feet after every step is essential to avoid slipping, using the poles as an aid for support.

Now below us as well, there is a steady stream of torch lights, following us up the slopes, winding up the slope like a snake, lights in single file. After a couple of hours of this, despite the goal so near in our sight now, this is monotonous, boring, slow, and a dark mood comes over me – there could be another six or seven hours of this. The longer it goes on, the more I feel if I could get back to the campsite by myself, I would about turn and head home. Rod does not do queues.

So after we have been walking for some time, it is time for a longer break, water and to catch our breath. This part has been steep and has been quite vigorous. Everyone is very quiet. Jeff and Chris are not struggling with the temperature with their fewer layers, and to be honest, with the wind chill still not as predicted, if my feet and hands do feel slightly chilly, my body doesn't and I could quite happily lose a layer. But for the time being I will stick as I am, I can't see it getting any warmer for a while!

We are off again, having readjusted our clothing and with that incessant trail of lights above and below, pole, pole. Through one stop and another we have been overtaken by the odd group or two, and then as they stop we get in front of them again. William can't be enjoying this pace either, as he gets us to leave the main trail and we start climbing quicker to the side of this, quicker than most other parties. We are now walking along a rocky ridge and have created some space for ourselves, some of the monotony of the queue has gone. But with this increase in pace comes the extra exertion of the body and one can now feel the heart rate, even hear the heart rate quicken, especially when we have high steps ups along the ridge, and at times now I can feel quite breathless. Conversation stops as it is head down and drive yourself on. This is hard as a tremendous amount of willpower is now needed. Chunga ranges up and down our line, checking on us, seeing if we are coping, and it is as much as one can manage to just smile and nod as he comes along side to check on your welfare.

We have escaped the crowd, we have been going some four hours – but if only we could stop for a rest, as we are all beginning to suffer, Claire, Neil, and I in silence, Jeff and Chris more vociferously. The cold is just starting to creep in a little, mainly my feet, not uncomfortable, but yes, I am just starting to feel it. Jeff and Chris continue their protestations, but William says we must go on. The trail is now a series of switchbacks and we reach a point where we are more sheltered by taller rocks, then Chris throws his dummy out of the pram and says he is stopping regardless (how good he is at speaking for all of us). William has to bow to his decision, "mutiny in the ranks" for the first and only time on this trip, but the effect our pace now will have on us will be seen later.

I am very grateful for the stop, though I have come through the dark mood of a couple of hours ago, the queues etc., and would have pushed myself on, it is nice just to stop and feel cardiac function return a bit back to normal. A suitable point to disappear behind a rock, and enough privacy for Claire as well.

After that welcome stop for all of us, and with the likes of Sugar Ray providing entertainment, a smile, and encouragement, we proceed along this zigzag up the side of Kili in the dark, and by far this is the hardest climbing we have done on the trip (Barranco Wall though steeper, seems like a doddle compared with this dark rarefied atmosphere). We have passed 5000 metres some time ago, a long time ago. We are now more exposed to the elements, though the wind is still being kind to us. But the drudgery continues as we plod on in the dark, so we cannot see our target getting closer. The repetition continues; we get higher and higher and we are now all in our own little worlds, but if there is a difference now, whereas before Claire and I were bringing up the rear, there is a change in batting order as we and Neil are now the front runners. But it is in silence we continue as we struggle for breath, often one foot down, stop, breath, and on again, repeating the process over and over again.

Slowly but surely night starts to lift, daybreak approaches and one of the porters comes to dim my torch, we can just about see each step without the use of artificial light now. The zigzags stop and now it is a hard slog uphill over rocks, scree and now for the first time in any appreciable amount, some snow. I don't feel that cold now, as we approach a ridge we have seen above us for some time.

I am (to be honest) at this point a bit in a world of my own, very tired, the lack of sleep over the past few days now feeling as if it has caught up with me, well overtaken me as well. This has been hard, very hard, mainly because of the monotony of walking for so long in the dark. Below us is the whole of Africa and we can't see any of it. Now this ridge doesn't seem to end, as I follow Claire and William on up it. As we continue to scramble up the slope, the first signs of the sun begin to appear, and with it a little more warmth. We have a glacier on our left, the Rebmann Glacier, and in front of us a rocky point. We turn a corner round this and William says to stop – time for a break – a well-earned break for a few minutes.

From nowhere, we have arrived at Stella Point, 5752 metres above sea level. It can't have been so monotonous after all, because I thought we had still a way to go. We are at the point by ourselves, where has everyone else gone? William, Claire, myself, then Neil and Chris arrive with one porter. What a star, out of nowhere he produces a flask of tea for us to share, and I find that well-travelled Kendal Mint Cake to share amongst us.

We are exhausted, but knowing our goal is near, we start to talk again, but as we stay there longer we find we have lost Jeff, and with him, Chunga, Sugar Ray, and Loderick. We have our snack, hoping they will come round the corner, but no, and we have no idea what has happened. In the solitude of the last part of the walk where we were driving ourselves on in our self-contained worlds, he was there then he wasn't. None of us had noticed. There was a sense of disappointment amongst us, as we had bonded so well that we all wanted to succeed together, the sense that if one of us failed then we all had.

And with our arrival at Stella Point, Neil, who has been in good spirits as we get here, is now also suffering, having disappeared briefly behind a rock to throw up, and was feeling a little dizzy again – the return of altitude sickness to him. It is only now that we have stopped to regroup that we can see how each other is faring. The other three of us are fine, but how we would have been now if Chris hadn't forced that stop earlier on us, we shall never know. I suspect we would have been a lot worse than just the tiredness that we feel.

I have been told that this part of my story lacks the enthusiasm of before, comes across as unexciting and being somewhat down in spirits. Perhaps this is the part of the climb that before departing, my friend who said he had hated the climb was referring to, with just a procession of lines of people trailing up the mountain. For me, I can only reiterate what I have already said, and it has been said by others who have done the climb as well, that this part does seem a dark place where you are wrapped up in yourself, and totally oblivious to anything around you. Perhaps that is why we didn't notice that Jeff was no longer with us. In a nutshell, we had arrived at this point after a nearly six-hour walk in the dark, only seeing the footstep in front of us by torchlight, plus the occasional look up to see the lines of lights above us. I felt alone, pushing myself to the limit in these inhospitable surrounds of rock, ice, and cold (and it could have been a lot colder, we were spoilt with that). It was monotonous, even with our goal slowly getting nearer. As I have said before, I could have easily turned around purely from that monotony. It required a lot of effort to put one foot in front of another, and go up as well, sometimes with large steps up, and with the lack of oxygen, this was very demanding on body and mind, and even pole, pole, talking required too much energy. Talk or breathe, the choice was easy. Perhaps it would have been "easier" if we had been able to see the views around us. I fancy it would have been. But the aim was to climb to the summit for sunrise, and now that time is approaching.

We have to push on, with or without Jeff. It is time to collect ourselves together now, to tackle the last part of our quest, in altitude terms, another 200 metres up to the summit.

Stella Point is on the edge of the volcanic crater, so our journey will now take us along the edge of the crater until we reach the highest point. Four of us, William and our trusty porter emerge from around the rock at the Point and there in the distance in front of us is our goal. And there too are some of the people who had disappeared from our sight; we had not seen anyone else now for some time. Some of them going, the last few yards, sorry, metres to the peak, some at the peak, and some starting their journey down again.

The final push takes us up a gentler slope, but we are now walking in up to nine inches of snow, which will have thawed a little yesterday, with many footprints in it; it had now refrozen, making walking quite hard. We should also not forget the altitude, so it is still necessary to take it steady, and we have to get Neil there now he is so close, but suffering.

It is time to reflect on this final push, the achievement of a lifetime's ambition, now it is so close – of my successes and failures in life, Lindsay, Davina, work, Mum worrying about me up here, of the encouragement I have received from the likes of Graham, Margaret, Sally, Jenny, and Dave to mention but a few, who had all pushed me, encouraged me when my enthusiasm was perhaps flagging. The camaraderie we have developed between each other on the trek (but a sadness that Jeff is now not with us and we will not do it together). If I hadn't achieved this by the time I was fifty, I AM going to do it, and it is so close now.

The passing groups we see look elated as they start their descent and offer us congratulations as we will soon be there for our final few steps. We are surrounded by snow now, to our left the spectacular Southern Ice Fields, the site of glaciers, and standing out in glittering white as the sun gives off more and more light.

So close now, there will be no stopping until we are there, at Uhuru Peak, and that forty-minute walk from Stella is nearly completed; it gets closer and closer, step by step.

Groups await their turns in front of us to do their photo shoots at the summit, one gets off and another takes its place.

Sadly there is no race between Jeff and Neil to get there first, but fittingly it will be Claire who has turned out to be our strongman in the party, offering encouragement to all, who will be the first of us, myself, Chris and Neil, we have done it.

At 06.35 hours, July 5th 2012, I reach the summit, I AM AT UHURU PEAK. 5895 metres (19341 feet) with the whole of Africa below me. I – we – HAVE DONE IT! I have achieved a lifetime ambition, to stand at the roof of Africa. So the four of us rejoice, a hug with Claire, handshakes with Chris, and Neil, and a special thank you to William for guiding us here. What a pity that Chunga is not here as well, it has been his trip and it would have been nice to celebrate with him, and of course Jeff as well.

We have to wait our turn to stand on the rocks that represent the peak, with its new sign, 'CONGRATULATIONS, You are now at UHURU PEAK', etc. So I have a bit of time to take in the views below us. To the south, the impressive Heim, Kersten, and Decken Glaciers, those spectacular columns of ice standing side by side, towards the Western Breach behind the new sign, and to the north dipping below us over the ridge of the crater a snow-covered terrain leading to the Reusch Crater, and contained within it, the Ash Pit, a sign of the old volcano. As the sun is now rising fast, this panorama is truly a magnificent sight.

And now it is our turn to stand on the summit, to archive our achievement with photos of the whole group with porters, the four of us, and individual pictures, and of course one of Claire and Chris together. I was told or had read, that the sense of achievement when you get to this point, the sense of elation, overcomes the tiredness that you feel, but at this stage, I am exhausted and my summit photo reflects this in my face. I am knackered! Our pictures done, it is time to take in what's around me again. Chris and Claire relax, sitting on the side of the monument, Neil is now really starting to suffer again, and I have a chance to absorb all around, the sun continuing to rise fully in the east, and with it a red/yellow hue beginning to spread over the skyline.

Six thirty-five in the morning was our summit time; we are here nearly two hours earlier than we had expected to be. For me, a blessing in that it had shortened the monotony of this part of the climb in the dark, but perhaps it had taken its toll especially on Jeff and Neil.

All parties only have a limited time up here, partly because of the constant train of other climbers arriving, and partly of course because of the effects at this altitude on the body, so we are told we have another five minutes, then we must start to return. And with this, a last look round, I can only reflect on this magnificent treasure that Tanzania has, a treasure now in my life, and that as a country they must look after it. If the ice is slowly melting, how long will these glaciers remain? The constant tread of feet and erosion, how will this affect the mountain? And, it is an untidy place, so much litter left on the slopes, rather than being removed by those that have taken it there.

Visibility is now very good, the weather has been very kind to us, and the wind-chill never what was expected, although it did get cold at times. But, in my Michelin layers, I never really felt it. In the ever-increasing warmth now, it is time to go and from here it is, literally, all downhill. All those days of climbing for twenty minutes at the top, and in not much more than twenty-four hours we will be back at the hotel. Behind William, we are in line again and the six of us leave the summit, back through the frozen footsteps in the snow towards Stella Point. The trail in front of us is getting increasingly busier as that earlier torchlight procession nears its goal.

And as we are back on the move, after some twenty minutes I look ahead and there is Jeff, being helped by

Chunga, Sugar Ray and Loderick, looking shattered, drained, coat undone, but he is going to do it. Fantastic, how good does that make me feel that, yes, we all will achieve what we set out to do? I really thought they had turned back with him. This will make the evening better. A shake of hands with Chunga, and we continue in our opposite directions, but we will meet up again in the not too distant future, to descend together.

We continue to Stella Point and then bear left along the ridge a little further towards Gillman's Point, signposted, and past a large boulder named Bismark Towers. From here we have a choice, following the zigzag we ascended earlier, or taking the straight descent down through gravel slopes to the east side of this. Part of the reason for an early ascent, other than reaching our goal at sunrise, is to reach and do this descent before the ever- increasing warmth of the sun thaws this slope so the gravel slides and dislodges more. This slope is our chosen route, but as we are nearing it, Claire and myself are becoming increasingly concerned about Neil who is becoming more distressed, walking more erratically and doesn't look good. We are travelling at quite a pace now, where has pole, pole gone? So we raise our alarm with William. He makes us press on, faster but despite our protestations that we should stop, Claire is getting quite insistent, and I also state my concerns, but we are made to press on. Neil is in no state to argue the toss. Events then take themselves into their own hands – Neil stutters, staggers, and collapses. William and our other porter pick him up, one of his arms over one of their shoulders, and with one carrying his rucksack, they start running him down the slope. We think they should rest, but on reflection they are the ones with experience of altitude sickness, and that experience tells them to get him down to a lower altitude as quickly as possible. It can be a killer and Neil's predicament is serious.

So with Jeff, Chunga, and Sugar Ray behind us still, and three "running" down the slope, and Loderick trying to catch us up, it leaves Claire, Chris and I by ourselves, going down these gravelly slopes, mainly in a zigzag line to ease the strain on knees and ankles. I am now getting hotter and hotter, as the sun gives out more and more warmth, but without taking my boots off, I can't shed any layers over my legs, I can only start removing upper garments, gloves and hat to stow away in my rucksack. With the occasional stop for sippi sippi, our rapid descent continues, Neil in front still being run down the slope. Wonderful views now to one side the ridge we had climbed earlier, to the other a magnificent view of the open spaces to, and then Mawenzi rising high above them. Above us we can now see Jeff in view some way behind us, but we are nearly as one again, as it were, as Chunga and Sugar Ray increase his pace down to better oxygenated air. Chris is a little behind Claire and I, now with Loderick, intent on a discussion about his music, and doing his impression of disco dancing, not the best idea on these slopes, when yet again he falls, hurting his hip as he does so. We are falling like flies, but Chris can continue, though more slowly. Claire and I are now on our own, left to our own devices in this heat.

At least now, though we can see people ascending above us on the ridge, we seem alone on this downward run, and we can now see now see Barafu Hut in the distance getting closer and closer – we have some direction. I am sweating buckets in this heat, and feeling more and more tired, but the end of our first stage of the day is in sight, and as I am feeling increasingly tired, a rest in camp before we continue down to Millenium Camp will be most welcome. We turn towards the rocky surrounds above the camp, the two of us now, the others in our wake will be along soon, off the gravel and back onto the rocky path leading us into a far emptier campsite than we left, rounding deserted tents, and the new pitches as the next arrivals reach here, their ascent tomorrow.

In front of us at last, our tents, with our camp porters waiting there to clap us in, mutual handshakes all round as they share our sense of achievement, and with that, a very welcome drink of orange squash for us. A smile between the two of us, we enjoy our drink while we wait for the others one by one to arrive back themselves, smiles, handshakes, yes we have all done it. It is now but just gone 9.30, 9.45, and we have been up and back down again, and all relatively intact. Jeff and Neil now look a lot better in themselves, Chris okay. Mission accomplished.

Rigorous, hard, and at times monotonous especially in those early queues, but achieved, and now it is peaceful; where all those other people have disappeared to I don't know. We now have a bit of time to rest, pack our stuff that we left out in the tents last night, and thankfully at last get out of these long johns and waterproof trousers to cool down. I sit down in my tent, and as my phone does work from here, send a few texts back to England, to say yes, I've done it and am now on my way back down again. Then having done all that, I change my clothing into what I will wear to continue our descent a little later on, kneeling to continue to pack.

No, no, no, as I do so, I can feel my muscles in my calves tighten right up – possibly cramp and it is getting worse, and we still have some hours to walk when we set off again. This is no fun. Painfully, I manage to pack the rest of my kit, but just moving is uncomfortable and after doing the finishing touches, packing my rucksack, all I can do is just sit there, legs outstretched, hoping this will pass. Certainly rubbing them does not seem to make a difference.

We are having an early lunch before we will continue to descend down to Millennium Camp, so with much difficulty I get up out of the tent to meet up with the others outside our mess tent, so our tents can be taken down ready for the off. By now the camp is streaming with new arrivals, including our GI, double amputee, the best of luck to him. Another large party of forty or so Americans stop by our tent, and a couple of them are interested in whether we have done the summit yet, and what it was like. I am quiet, my cramp easing slowly as I am able to stretch and stand on my legs. Is this a combination of the high salt meal last night, and not being able to take some of my clothing off when coming down? I was sweating a lot and coming downhill so fast, a very different motion to our climb over the past few days. Just a theory. I am worried about the rest of today, but I am happier on my feet, rucksack and poles by my side.

A leisurely lunch is taken while we recover from our exertions of earlier, a good-sized meal to replace some of the calories we have already expended today so far. We are now more relaxed and talkative than earlier in the day, and can now reflect on our success. Appetites are good as we clear most of what is put in front of us. While we eat, our camp is taken down ready to go on its journey down, the porters' job nearly done.

As we emerge from the tent, ready to start walking again, the wind is getting up and it has now clouded over, perhaps now the dullest it has been since the afternoon descending down to Shira. Sitting down, I have started to cramp up a little again, but hopefully a slow walk will ease my muscles. I hope so, otherwise this could be a painful afternoon. I go to where I left my rucksack, to find that someone has stolen my poles, which is quite upsetting. It had to be the party of Americans walking by before we went into the tent.

Resigned to my loss as there are now so many people about, Peter (the camp leader) lends me one of his poles, William another, but they are larger than mine.

We have a walk of two, two and a half hours down to Millennium Camp descending down to 3790 metres. We set off back down the ridge that we had entered Barafu from yesterday, on what is probably the steepest part of this walk. Then instead of bearing west back towards Karanga and back down the switchbacks up onto this ridge, we continue along it further until we reach a point where the landscape starts to flatten out more to a less steep gradient, and we start to trek across the plateau below the volcano.

The sun has gone, and it is now very dull as we cross this

dusty landscape, taking it steady at the back as my legs slowly start to feel more comfortable. Dust turns to rock, and then we start seeing a return of some vegetation again, the first since the Karanga valley as we return to a moorland landscape again. Heathers/giant heathers become more common.

Jeff and Neil are still having their rucksacks carried for them, but at least they are feeling better, Chris is still a little sore from his fall, and Claire as strong as ever. It really has gone dull now, and there is more wind as the mountain peak gets further and further behind us. It won't be so nice up there now. Chunga comes over for a chat, and has heard over their walkie-talkie that word has come down from the last campsite, Barafu, that Peter has retrieved my poles for me. That is good, wonderful news. I certainly wouldn't argue with this guy if confronted by him.

This trudge over dusty rocks goes on as we continue gently downwards, as we approach the forest edge, not thick vegetation, but more and more scrub, taller with especially large heathers, what a variety of scenery we have walked through today – rock (in the dark), snow fields, moorland and heathland and now thin forest. After just over two hours' walking we enter a clearing amongst the heathers, split in two by a line of them, one smaller area and one quite large, flat space with huts at one end. After fourteen hours, we enter Millennium Camp and our work is done for the day, time to put our feet up for a well-earned rest.

Our arrival is not that far behind the porters, so our camp is still being set up in the smaller area, a clearing amongst the heathers, but as is the fashion of the past few days, now water is available again, our bowls and hot water are produced, and we have a welcome and thorough wash. We are all well covered in a layer of dust especially from the descent down from Bismark Towers. Even I have gone two days without shaving, and it is time to remove some stubble. And, bless them again, that welcome hot drink appears as well. As this is drunk, we indulge in pure luxury as we take the opportunity of bathing our feet, leaving them to soak in the warm water, finding a nice earth ledge to sit on whilst doing this. We have some time to ourselves now, the tents are up and we can read, sleep, or do whatever we want to for the afternoon. I unpack for the last time in the tent, write a few notes on today and read my book. I will hopefully doze for a bit before we will join each other for our last camp supper. We had been given nuts to help ourselves to when we arrived in camp, again to rebuild our energy reserves, and we will eat in a couple of hours, meeting up before the meal, when we have to decide what remuneration we are to give to our support crew, the money that Chunga had collected off us back at the hotel over a week ago.

I lie quietly in my tent, the rest of the site quiet as well. I can reflect on the day, though it still hasn't really sunk in as to what I have achieved for myself. I have had a couple of texts back from England congratulating me on achieving that ambition.

Some noise as another party arrives at the campsite, settling down across the other side of the large clearing; they couldn't be further away from us, but I am surprised there are not more arrivals, for the number that would have summited today (though the descent route is not the same for everyone, depending on which ascent route was taken).

I probably do doze for a while, more than I have done over the past few days, relax, and then meet the others for a chat and drink (soft, that is). There are set rates for the different jobs that different porters do, so with our agreement, Chunga goes through these rates, and we agree on those rates, acknowledging the wonderful work they have all done and how much we have appreciated them. One by one we go through them, agreeing on the right remuneration, not of course forgetting the driver who picked us up from the airport and took us to the start of the trek. We find after all this that we have a surplus, but after discussing the merits of each and every one, we decide we will split it equally amongst all. Chris is nominated as our paymaster, to hand the money out in the morning.

Supper now follows and we are not let down with our last full meal in our camp on the mountain. We are all in good spirits, the others have caught up on some sleep and Jeff and Neil feel fine – you would not know now they had been troubled on the mountain. Chunga is in good humour and we are giving him a lot of stick about this and that, and more seriously of what his plans are for his future. We now know that when he has finished eating with us, he then goes and joins the porters for further refreshment, so we tease him by offering him every spare scrap that we have not eaten ourselves. Indeed we have had a good laugh over supper.

But then our mood is tempered by the news over the bush telegraph that as we have all succeeded today, a man from another party had died on the mountain today after being taken ill with altitude sickness; he could not be got down the mountain quickly enough, and was taken to the wrong camp to get assistance, where there were not the right facilities to help him. His wife had carried on to the summit, thinking all would be okay, a sad return for her for the news she would receive on her descent. The mountain will not lay itself open with ease to all, and to us underlined the risks that both Neil and Jeff could have gone through earlier today, and of Loderick carrying that oxygen bottle all the way with us. Yes, William did know best when he pushed us hard back to Stella Point and beyond on the way down.

There is then a commotion on the other side of the camp, which we find was due to a couple of new porters in their party stealing from their walkers, and hiding their booty. On discovery of their crimes, swift retribution was handed out by the camp leader, and the long-term prospects of these two as roles as porters and a future better life would now be over.

We have been very lucky with our crew, I couldn't praise them more.

Chunga leaves us to top up his calories in the other tent, and we chat for a while about our day before retiring to our tents, a last night under canvas.

A short read, and then as it gets colder, I snuggle back down into my sleeping bag after a long and fulfilling day, and try to sleep. It has taken me this long to find out how best to make myself comfortable and as I close my eyes, even if sleep does not come readily, I can be very satisfied with my day, my week on the mountain.

I've done it. 06.35, July 5th 2012.

Sunrise over Kili's crater, the Ash Pit behind me.

The retreating glaciers near the summit, above the clouds behind.

16. MILLENNIUM CAMP TO MWEKA GATE, AND BEYOND

Today we return back to our hotel, our walk will be over. We will carry on rapidly down, reaching Mweka Gate, and then will return to Moshi by road again, then return back to the hotel to unwind and even have the luxury of a decent bath or shower.

Our last day in camp starts as usual at just after six, when – yes, I did get a little sleep – I rise and start my final packing while I wait for that cup of coffee to come for the last time. The usual routine, I am waiting as I hear it arrive outside, ready to greet my "waiter" and unzip the tent to get my warm drink. I dress, wash, and prepare for breakfast. We convene in the tent, where our porridge and cooked breakfast is brought for us, gratefully received as ever. Chunga as usual eats with us, and tells us we will meet up with our crew in a few minutes, when they have done a little of the clearing up after the meal, the final clear up for them as well.

The sun is out and we congregate outside the tent, as one by one the porters join us, breaking from their jobs. For once, it is not them and us as we mingle with each other waiting for Chunga and William to come. We are all here, smiles all around, as one by one Chunga calls a porter forward and Chris gives him his tip from us. They shake our hands in turn, and then the next one until we have given everyone our little tip for all their hard work in helping us. Chunga tells them that there is a surplus but it is our wish that it be divided out equally between them all. They clap and thank us again. When all is completed, there is much joy, and they go into their Tanzanian greeting song, and ritual dancing. Us, we clap them and enjoy their celebrations, a repeat of the greeting they gave us at Shira those few days ago, but now we have become friends, we know each other better, and are able to join in with them. And, if we haven't heard it enough over the past few days, more Bob Marley from William. They have all been absolutely fantastic, friendly, helpful, always smiling and from nowhere, Peter retrieved my poles. Sugar Ray has been a laugh, Loderick was quieter but had a calming effect on us, always there in the background, and always there to talk to. We can't thank them enough, to them what we have given them in Tanzanian terms is a lot, but it seems scant reward in English terms for all their efforts in helping us.

It is time to move. The tents need to be taken down, the camp cleared, and we, we need to be getting down the mountain. It is eight o'clock, and we are ready to go; we say our goodbyes because this is the last we will see of them.

It has snowed overnight on the mountain, the wind has got up and the early sunshine gone. We head off down the trail – it looks well used, almost like a track as we set off through the heather-surrounded route. We will walk for some four hours back to the pickup point, and it will all be downhill so hard on my knees. We haven't gone very far before the scenery changes, giant heathers and then Protea surround us on our dusty way, a hard rocky path and the gradient down is staring to increase. We are now far more enclosed as the open moorland distances itself behind us. Loderick is leading us now, with Chunga and William bringing up the rear, deep in conversation. He is having his assessment for promotion and I don't know if this is what they are talking about. As the descent continues and becomes more slippery, whether through muddy places or dust on smooth rock, a side bet is suggested that whoever slips over first will have to buy the first round tonight when we have returned to civilisation. Chris is the odds-on favourite. We go at a fairly brisk pace – altitude is not a problem now, only the conditions underfoot, and the joints of us old men, Chris and

I chatting as the others motor on down. We approach another camp, Mweka Huts at 3106 metres, a busy campsite teeming with other trekkers also on their descent, but as yet, not underway. This site looks quite posh, with proper toilet units (apparently with a new decomposition system, greener and more efficient, and if successful will be installed on other sites).

Other than a quick drink of water, we pass swiftly on and it is not very far before again we return to rainforest, cloud forest starting as a well-defined line between heather and these tall trees that now surround us. These tress are thick-trunked and covered in moss and lichen, reaching high towards the sky. It is more humid, misty but warm – a far different environment from what we have seen before. And with this, it is now far muddier underfoot. I had read before we left about the state of the paths here, so having pre-warned myself, I take extra care. A previous path has become rutted, so deep that another path has been built beside it, with a lot of effort to make steps out of timbers, but this doesn't make walking any easier as you are continually having to adjust your stride pattern. Some of this descent is quite steep. We will descend nearly 1500 metres to Mweka Gate and our lift, and in not much more than two hours, so the descent is quick.

Jeff loses the bet, slipping over first, well actually the only one to, and dirtying himself with the mud.

We do see the occasional porter going up, a small group, a couple of armed militia, and a couple of locals with machetes, what they are doing even Chunga doesn't know. Otherwise it is very quiet. The path turns into a track and we are able to walk side by side, the youngsters out in front of us. Chris and I take the opportunity to have a proper chat with Chunga about his country, his people, and his ambitions and of local politics. There is some political stability, but the infrastructure of the country needs developing. Tribal warfare has diminished and through government co-operatives there is some development in the country's agriculture. He obviously loves his country. He continues to tell us his aspirations, the hope that he can save enough money to start his own tour guide company in the not too distant future. We can only wish him luck and thank him for his guidance with us.

We continue to chat and then in low cloud at the edge of the rainforest, we come to the end of our walk – we have arrived at Mweka Gate. Our jeep is waiting for us, and our luggage has already been brought down by the boys. Mweka Gate is a small hamlet on the edge of the forest, just outside Moshi. There are several shops, bars, and a registration hut that we have to sign off at, to say that we have completed our journey and come down safely.

Having seen nothing but dust for a few days, the last part of the walk has meant our boots are now covered with mud, and we are surrounded by a host of village children, equipped with brushes, wanting to clean our boots for a small remittance, two dollars. Which one do you give the money to, to help their poverty? It doesn't seem fair to pick one, I will get them done at the hotel properly so I can pack them dry and clean.

It's eleven thirty, we have come down quickly, and our walking is finished. My calves now ache from all the downhill work, 7000 feet in that short time. How a Kili beer would go down now!

There is a wait while William organises the certificates, which are not forthcoming so he decides he will stay behind to wait for them. We are given the choice of lunch back at the hotel, or at somewhere called The Glacier Club, the place to be in Moshi, the latter our unanimous choice.

We board the jeep and head down the road towards town, passing our porters loading their stuff onto their bus. A final wave to them, again they have been wonderful; a couple of them may join us later, although Sugar Ray has apparently already started back up the mountain with another party.

As we continue down this road, it is back to reality as we

pass huts, small houses, with the people's subsistence living obvious: pigs, goats in pens around these habitations, them trying to scratch out a living. The further we go, the more affluent it seems as the standard of agriculture improves, lots of coffee plantations either side of the road before entering the outskirts of Moshi. We stop outside two large, solid metal gates with a walled surround, The Glacier Club, deserted but opened up for us. There is a huge lawn, surrounded by a dance area, a couple of open air restaurants and bars. This is the place to be in Moshi on a Friday or Saturday night, and today is Friday.

Lower down now, the clouds have dispersed and the sun is shining. That Kilimanjaro beer that I have been dreaming about for days is now in front of me. Nectar.

We feel quite relaxed now after our hard week, probably smelly, dirty, aching limbs and in serious need of a bath, but, it is good to sit and enjoy each other's company as we have become one, and talk turns to home and Jeff's trip to Zanzibar tomorrow (lucky bugger!).

A wonderful meal is prepared for us on the barbeque, light but very good and enjoyed by all. It will soon be time to return to the hotel, but first a man from Ashanti Tours arrives to bring us back our valuables, stored these past few days in their safe, and he is going to get some smaller denomination dollars for us as well.

Time to take a Kili beer out onto the lawn, and relax in the sunshine, while we wait. There, appearing between the trees is the real Kilimanjaro, in all his magnificence, smiling down on us now. Yesterday we were at the top, an ambition fulfilled, but too exhausted to enjoy it, to take it in. But now, today, twenty-four hours later, I can sit back and take it in – yes, I really did it. It is starting to sink in, what I pushed my way through, and achieved. It is a brilliant feeling and something I won't forget for a very long time. Eight days ago we saw the snow-covered peak from the hotel appearing out of the clouds, we lost sight for a couple of days as we started through the rainforest, and then reappeared as we crossed the Shira Plateau to remain in our sights until we were on top. That long, steep walk to Stella Point, then to Uhuru Peak, and now back to the bottom. What a sight again, and a lasting memory, and with that the emotions I now feel for what I have done.

Enough of that. Our money changed, it is back to the hotel in the jeep where we receive a warm welcome from all the staff. What friendly people these are. We are shown to our rooms, a different block to the one I was in on arrival, but upstairs again, overlooking the pool. I hand over my boots in at reception to be cleaned, and pick up the bag I had left there. Back in the room I unpack everything and lay it all out on the shelves, including those ginger biscuits I have carried from Telford, through Heathrow, up to Uhuru Peak and down again – perhaps at the airport tomorrow they will fill a gap.

My first look in the mirror, not as bad as I thought, so decisions, pool or shower. A no-brainer, I find my swimming things and a towel and head off down to the pool, where Jeff and Neil have already arrived. The water looks inviting so I dive in, enjoy a few lengths, and enjoying the cool of the water. Chris and Claire are now with us, they have a table under a tree so I join them to talk, have a drink, and unwind. I stick to Coke as we will be returning to The Glacier Club later to spend the evening. Around the pool it really is a lovely setting and a fitting place to relax, with the view of Kili between the trees behind us. The sun shines, it is hot and all is well with the world. The way we have all bonded and enjoy each other's company has been fantastic and probably wouldn't have happened if our party was larger. I sit back and relax and enjoy. Later we will think about getting ready to go out, about packing, and we must decide between us how much to give Chunga. I have already asked if I could speak tonight as it was a lifetime ambition, and had sort of planned a speech while coming down the mountain earlier.

I go back to the room, put the sleeping bag and fleece out to air on the balcony and then I sort through the clothes that I am going to leave for the Porters Trust, put all the medicines together, and the food, and then it is time to get ready for tonight. A proper shower at last, bliss, and a mirror to shave at properly, clean at last.

We are going to meet in the hotel lobby at seven, so I do have a bit of time to chill, and to start my packing, before getting dressed and going down. I am first as usual, with a wait for Jeff and Neil, who are preening, but we board the jeep with Chunga and the local boss from Ashanti Tours. A late night is in prospect. As we leave it is warm and darkness descends, bringing us a wonderful starlit night. Arriving at The Glacier Club by seven thirty, it is quite quiet at the moment.

A table and chairs has been put out on the lawn for us, with a barbeque close by, our personal chef in tow. We make jokes about which paper Chris worked for, something Neil initiated. We are in flippant mood. Beers are ordered; I like this Kili beer so will stick with this, along with Chunga. The others try another African beer. The barbeque is lit and we enjoy the warmth of the evening before our meal is served. Soup then chicken cooked on our oven, nice but a little tough (actually it was better on the mountain), but who cares? It is our last night together in Africa and we are going to enjoy it. King William arrives with a couple of the other porters, he has got our certificates now. He also seems far more relaxed now we are down off the mountain.

More beers and then it is time for Chunga to make a little speech, before giving out our certificates with a little extra on his thoughts on each of us, me he thought quiet and a worrier (though my questions to him were more trying to find out more about the mountain). He finishes and I reply to him on behalf of the five of us. I had already collected his "reward" from the others. My lifelong ambition of climbing to the

Roof of Africa had been achieved, I began, and would go on to thank the others for their wonderful company, to say I felt if one had failed we would have all felt a sense of failure, how my friends would be envious that I had done the walk with the "chief rugby correspondent of the Sun", and that when Chris and Claire had finished their respective careers, they could consider doing a Punch and Judy show on Clevedon beach – that brought a laugh. A special thanks to Claire who had looked after us so well when we were suffering and driven us on. And then to Chunga, a wonderful leader for us to have, his steadying words that everything was normal or level (an in-joke). A toast to us all, for Chris and Jeff, slippy slippy, to us all, as Chunga would say, sippi sippi. I shake his hand, his tip placed in his grasp.

By now the club is filling up, a reggae band is playing, people are on the dance floor and they have lit a fire near us in a hollow on the lawn, with massive logs that will keep us warm for some time. Jeff and Chris are in deep conversation on the loyalty of the soldier to Queen, country or regiment, and then onto the monarchy or a republic, all very intense for this time of night. Chunga wants to dance, Claire is fighting with a piece of chicken stuck between her teeth, Neil is after another beer, and he too is up for dancing now, so he and Chunga head off to the dance floor. As the others are still deep in discussion, I wander over to join them, though reggae is not really, and never will be my sort of music. Anyway we try, but we are not up to the standard of Tanzanian movement, and one or two random blokes come up and dance with us – help! It passes the evening away while the band plays on, but then they finish after a couple of encores, so we leave the dance floor and go back with the others to settle up for our beer. A disco starts up, more my type of music, but by now it is past midnight and it has been a long, but enjoyable day, so after listening to a bit of the disco, we find the jeep and return back to the hotel. Chunga and William look set for the night, staying behind at The Glacier, what state will they be in when we meet up later in the "now" morning!

Back at the hotel, it's late but we are two hours ahead of England so a phone home, expensive at £1.50 per minute, but nice to talk, and then at last a proper bed for the first time in a week.

Back to civilisation, a shave in front of a mirror, a shower for the first time in a week, and now a proper bed, but still a wonderful experience on the mountain. Lovely to get back to our creature comforts, what we are used to.

At some stage in the day after reaching Moshi, I think when Neil and I were sitting on the lawn at The Glacier Club, he asked me if I would do it again. My answer, no chance, I've done it and that's it. Now, sleep.

Back down through the rainforests.

This made it all worthwhile!

17. MOSHI AND HOME
JULY 7TH 2012

I've slept at last, but I stirred early and made myself a cup of coffee, which I take back to bed and read for a while. I really like the rooms in these blocks, I could almost live here if there was a kitchen as well, overlooking the lawn, and Kilimanjaro starring down at me. I enjoy the coffee (no tap on the door this morning with coffee delivery by my porter, we were spoilt up there), and then up to finish packing.

There was an option to go to the Game Reserve at Arusha, which I had hoped to do, to see some wildlife, especially elephants, and Chris and Claire had also expressed an interest in this. Yesterday as we drove back into Moshi from Mweka, we had discussed this again, but with a departure early afternoon, and Jeff leaving earlier to catch his flight to Zanzibar, we felt it would be too much of a rush. It would be nice to spend our last few hours all together. Plus of course I had no camera!

Chunga had offered to take us into Moshi for the morning, and to have lunch there, so that is what the five of us decided to do, with a more relaxed start to the day (the Game Reserve would have been another early rise), especially with a long trip back to Heathrow to endure. So it was arranged to meet up for breakfast at eight, a real lazy start compared with our time on the mountain.

Our last day together starts with us meeting for breakfast, and the order of appearance is the same as has been the whole week. Only two other guests are in the hotel, so it is greatly overstaffed, waiters falling over backwards to be helpful, to serve us cereals, fruit, beverages etc., but a cooked breakfast and coffee will do me fine whereas the others go for the full McCoy (it is such a lovely hotel, the Weru Weru River. I hope it becomes more popular so the lovely staff can be fully utilised, they can't do enough for you). We are enjoying what's in front of them when I say the wrong thing. Like Claire the previous evening, I had also trouble with parts of the spare ribs getting stuck between my teeth, but with the aid of a toothpick in the middle of the night, had managed to dislodge it. Poorly worded, I announced to Claire that I had managed to shift my meat in the middle of the night, and then admitting straight away "That came out wrong," only seemed to make it worse, but everyone was in fits of hysterics at my expense.

It was a really good breakfast but with our unknown itinerary for the next twenty-four hours, it could be our last decent meal of the day. The hotel had kindly said we need not vacate our rooms until our final departure from the hotel, meaning that we could leave all our luggage in them until our return from Moshi, allowing for a final change for the journey home. So, collecting the few things we need for our trip into town, we arrange to assemble in reception to await the arrival of Chunga and the jeep. I also take down with me the items I am going to donate to the Porters Trust.

Chunga, much to our surprise, has arrived at the time he said he would, saying he had had a good but not late night, but he hadn't returned to his home. William is with him in the jeep with our regular driver. We travel into Moshi, passing firstly through what looks a more prosperous and developed area, with some light industry, before turning into the main street, and then into a back street running parallel with this. This is more a dirt road, with huts and shacks beside it. Locals are plying their trade at whatever they can do to scratch a living, reconditioning tyres, turning old tyres into shoes, along with various souvenir shops, some selling local art. One has to remember that the mountain itself is probably the main source of income into the area. Chunga takes us to a shop that sells ornaments, local jewellery, then to other "arty" shops selling animals carved out of wood, paintings etc. I would like to take something back for my twenty-month-old granddaughter, but nothing is really suitable, with little sharp things that may fall out. Artists are painting pictures of the mountain and of wildlife while you watch, but if you look carefully, all they are doing is wetting their brushes and going over what has already been painted, but the others do indulge and buy one or two. Neil wants to buy his son a Tanzanian national football shirt but we can't find the right size. The locals are very friendly again and don't hassle us, they greet us as we pass and smile and go out of their way to try and find what we want but are not pushy if they have not got it. Once again, there don't seem many tourists about bar us.

We walk past a Barclays bank, and back into the main street which is quite busy. We go for an early lunch at a rather colonial-looking cafe, where Chris and Jeff launch into another deep and meaningful discussion, me joining in occasionally as we wait for our food to arrive. Many of the porters were also Manchester United fans, including William and Chunga, and I chat to Chunga about the team and Old Trafford, and if he ever got to England, it would be a pleasure to take him to a match there, to the ground. We also have a laugh about what happens if there is a local international game against Eritrea, in and out quick. To our surprise as we sit watching Moshi go by, one of the locals we had met only three quarters of an hour ago arrives with a football shirt, the right size for Neil to give to his son. You wouldn't get that sort of service back home would you! A bloke outside the cafe patrols the parking spaces with some powerful piece of gunnery in hand; back to the football discussion, dare we say shoot!

Our meals had arrived, but we had to wait an age for William's chips to arrive, but they do come and we enjoy a nice meal here, my chicken salad very good even if it did have lettuce (a good way to spoil a salad in my opinion). Our time is running out so we must sadly depart. We treat Chunga, William, and our driver to their lunch then it is time to board the jeep to return to the hotel for the last time. Jeff will leave an hour before us for his trip to Zanzibar, but we will not go to the airport with him and hang around, we will be taken there a bit later. I am largely packed, all I have to do really is gather my last few things together, and return to reception. I pick up my cleaned boots, what a fantastic job they have made of them, they look brand new, such a good job that I would have to admit that at the start of 2015, I still have not wanted to dirty them again after the job they have done.

So, all I have to do is check out – we have already tipped the staff from what we collected together at the start of the trip. The others meet me there, and sadly now it is the first of the goodbyes as Jeff's lift has arrived. Neil is taking some of his stuff back with him to England, one bag so Jeff can travel lighter. A pity we cannot travel back on block, but it has been great knowing Jeff and, he will forward me some photos when he returns to England.

Then there were four. A beer on the terrace will go down well, so we retire to the bar there and have a bit of banter with Chunga. I wander across the lawn one last time to see my mountain, Kilimanjaro, staring down on me – us – between the trees. Touching again, I did it, I really did it, I got to the top, and I achieved my lifetime ambition.

It's time to go, and our friendly staff are there to wave us farewell as we climb into the jeep one last time, start off through those big metal gates, and sadly it is farewell. I hope one day I will return, and nothing will have changed.

It is a quiet journey back to the airport, Chunga and William coming with us. Kilimanjaro towers over us to our right in glorious sunshine for most of the way back to the airport as if to say goodbye. It is about three o'clock when we get there, and unload our baggage. It is time to say goodbye to Chunga and William, and wish them well for the future, a sad moment so we shake of the hands with William, then a quick hug with Chunga. I cannot praise him enough for making this trip so memorable for me. William, it transpires from our comments, is not quite ready to be promoted up to a tour leader, and will do one more trip up the mountain before he can attain this. We wave goodbye as they depart from the airport.

Then it is time to queue up and check in, which does take some time as a lady with a thousand cases is in front of us, but we do eventually make it through into the departure lounge where we find a cafe to have a coffee. A passport control machine which checks fingerprints, and then we just sit, waiting until our flight is called. Jeff must have gone by now, and is supposed to text Neil upon his arrival in Zanzibar.

I read my book, nibbling at those well-travelled ginger biscuits, time going slowly as we wait for our plane to arrive from Mombasa. It does arrive eventually and we are called to our departure gate. A walk across the tarmac to board the plane, up the steps at the rear of the plane, and as before we enter the cabin, I turn to face the mountain for the last time.

This was probably the most moving part of the whole trip for me, the mountain, snow-covered, standing out in the pure blue sky, bathed in sunshine, standing behind the airport buildings. Over the past few days this mountain had become a part of my life, again an ambition achieved, and it was time to say goodbye. The emotion of it all came out at this moment. Delight, sadness, awe, respect. Over the past few days it had been my life and as it would turn out, would have a lasting effect on me. These were long seconds and if I held others up, this was something I had to do. But I promise myself that I will see my mountain again, but next time from the gamelands of the Serengeti, the Ngorongoro Crater. Yes, I must return to this wonderful part of Africa.

With those thoughts, those lasting memories, then perhaps this would be a good time to finish my story. I have succeeded in what I came to do, and everything may seem a bit of an anti-climax now. But even if the excitement of the past few days, anticipation, exertion, fulfilment is done, some of the rewards of the trip are still to come, bonds to make and also time to reflect. So with Kilimanjaro now behind me, with all that it has meant to me, time to go home. It has been a fantastic few days, hard but memorable. A real mix of emotions, determination and despite the strenuous walks, lack of sleep, neck problems, this has been a "holiday" and through all, there are many far worse off than us who have to endure hardship every day. But, for those in Tanzania, they always offered a smile and went out of their way to help. We have no impact on their lives, other than being part of their tourist industry, but they have made an impact on me. With that, the doors of the plane will close behind us and we will soon see the last of my mountain (this visit!) and I will continue my tale.

Onto the plane, and I am seated by Chris, but I have the window seat and will see the mountain a little while longer. We are ready to take off, homewards though this will be another long flight and another long stop over at Addis, before we return to Europe. A last long look at Kilimanjaro and Meru, the glaciers, the ice fields (how much longer will they be there?), the Western Breach, the people and the friendships, the experience and the fulfilment. All this will stay with me for a long time, and this is why I write this now.

As we now climb into the sky, levelling off and heading north-west, re-crossing the Equator, and flying back over Kenya it was time to get my book out again, until the in-flight meal was served. Then time to close my eyes as the sun starts to set over the arid lands of Northern Kenya and Ethiopia passes by below. By the time we have started to circle Addis Adiba darkness has fallen, but the city is seen in a better light than on the outward trip, so we can see the infrastructure, the main part of the capital, the main streets, rather than the slums on the outskirts observed previously. After a smooth landing, we disembark from the plane and onto a bus for the short journey to the new Terminal 1, a far grander building than the drab, uncomfortable Terminal 2 that we had spent those hours in flying out. Straight into the lounges, meeting all those other people waiting to fly out through the night. We found a row of seats where we could make our base, away from all the crowds, where we could relax with our hand luggage for that interminable time that we had to wait before catching our connection back to Heathrow, some six hours.

Claire was back in work mode, checking e-mails on her iPhone, Chris reading his book, and for all the time we had spent on the mountain together, I had never really got to know Neil that well, until now (the first time I suppose we had chatted away from Jeff). In those long hours we chatted about work, family, and really got to know each other better. He is another Man United fan so we chatted about the team, and prospects for the coming season, and I said if we kept in contact, then he would be quite welcome to use my season tickets at Old Trafford when I was not going. An interesting guy, and much more to him than I had thought previously. A very good sense of humour as well. He also managed to show me around his iPad, how he got books on the Kindle, and more in a language that being a technophobe like I am, I could understand. I was really pleased to have had this time with him.

One of us would go for a stroll from time to time, to stretch our legs, and for calls of nature. It was interesting to observe the diversity of people, cultures, Europeans, Asians, Africans, Arabs, as we all waited to go our own separate ways, how different cultures treated women, with some all waiting on their man. And again, the beauty of the Ethiopian Airline stewardesses, in their smart outfits, with their distinctive facial bone structure.

In time, the empty seat at the end of our road would be filled, an overlarge Arabian gentleman with his harem of women running around him, a lady, and then a tall, thin young man of Arab ethnicity. We thought nothing of this changing cycle of people, until after some twenty minutes of this gentleman leaving his seat, Neil had noticed that he had left his rucksack where he had been. We could see no sign of him anywhere. Should we be worried? The constant reminders we get on airport security and all that is said about unattended luggage, and here it is. Another ten minutes passed, and there was still no sign of his return, perhaps we should do something! Claire eventually got up in search of a security man, and on finding one returned and we explained about the bag being left – a bomb scare? What did he do? Well in the U.K. they probably would have evacuated the area, but no, he looked at the bag, picked it up, and ran off towards the security scanners with it. He disappeared, re-appeared, disappeared again for a while, before coming back over to us to tell us that they didn't think it was anything untoward. We described the man who had been sitting there as best we could and then the security man went off again.

After a while, we see him again with the bag and he is talking to an older (Arabic) gentleman in a check shirt. They went back and forth a couple of times before he was given the bag by the security man who had taken it from our seats. He came back over to explain to us that this man had reclaimed the rucksack, had been able to identify it and its contents correctly so they had given it back to him, so no problem. Fine, we said, but that was not the man who had left the bag there in the first place.

A mystery, and a bit of excitement for a few minutes amidst the drudgery of waiting for our departure. It was a long evening as the clock ticked on, onto Sunday, and we were finally called to our gate, queuing to go through security. A poor young family in front of us had to remove sleeping babies from their push chairs, and removed their own belts, shoes etc. to pass through, turmoil for them. And then another wait while disorganised queues formed and broke up as people impatiently waited to board their flight. In the end we found a seat and waited, who cares if we are last on?

SUNDAY:

It is past midnight, and the last day of adventure, though it will all be travelling. We had finally heard from Jeff, that he had safely arrived at his hotel in Zanzibar having suffered several delays, so his arrival had been considerably later than expected. Our departure is at five past one and it can't be long now before we are called after a couple of false alarms waiting with this impatient crowd. People watching distracted me from my reading, we will go when we are told, but people are so impatient. The call comes, but we wait to let the queue recede before we go through at our own pace, not having to wait anywhere. The people with the babies are still trying to manoeuvre themselves, offspring, and bags about – hard work.

Unfortunately for this part of the trip we were not seated together, Claire and Chris are opposite me, but even they have a woman between them. Neil, a window seat a couple of rows in front of me, seated next to a young lady who, as he tells us later, is a school teacher from Zimbabwe, and is an international hockey player (another hockey player) for them. I was seated next to a huge guy, occupying the window seat. He was an American naval guy, returning to the States via London from his ship in the Indian Ocean. What a long flight for him, and with no leg room for someone his size.

Time to settle down, go through the normal pre-take off stuff, safety belts on, and return to the skies. It was dark outside as we made our way down, taxiing down the runway to a stop. A rev of the engines and off we went, a smooth take-off into the night sky back towards London.

It was late now, and I suppose I thought that they would fed us sooner rather than later, so we could get some sleep, so I read for a while, then would try and close my eyes for a bit before the drive back home. I must say that I felt a bit cramped to with my little legs, so how must the guy next to me be feeling? We are offered a drink, but no food – it could be a monotonous flight – but hey, no screaming babies – yet! I do read quite a lot, my American colleague plays games on his laptop, but now sleep. The lights in the plane are dimmed, and I doze as we make our way further north-west. Yes, a baby does cry occasionally, but otherwise peace, and the occasional glance up at the monitor above, where we are and our estimated time of arrival in London. Over Egypt, the Med, Europe, and into French airspace – we are nearing home. For the final part of the flight I chat to my American colleague about anything and everything, his home, what I have been doing, but it sounds as if other than the navy, he is basically a small town guy.

Over the Channel, we are nearly there, and as one looks through the cabin window as the day breaks, it looks dull and cloudy, but then it is English summer. The final approach, altitude dropping and we touch down safely on the runway, brakes on, a smooth landing and we come to a halt, then taxi back to our disembarkation terminal. A cold, wet, dull and cloudy day to greet us on our return to the U.K. – it is the middle of our summer! I think it is supposed to be men's single finals day at Wimbledon today, Andy Murray playing Roger Federer. I hope the weather improves for the Olympics.

The four of us can now meet up again as we make our way to the long escalator that will take us towards luggage collection and passport control. We find our conveyor and wait, Neil having to look out for the bag he is taking for Jeff as well. A loo break while we wait, an interminable one for Claire at the ladies to the point she thinks of going in the gents, and then finally our luggage arrives.

This is a sad time, and I can only hope that at some date in the future we will meet up again, but for now, we will now go our separate ways. Neil doesn't have far to go, and if he gets back in time will go and see his son play schoolboy county cricket in the afternoon. Chris and Claire head back to Bristol, and me to Telford. We promise to keep in touch, hopefully meet up with Chris at or after some rugby game he may be covering, and have a beer together. Claire has collected all our e-mail addresses, and will forward me those of the others, and some of her photos. A shake of the hands, a hug, and they are gone. Neil and I wait while his bags appear, promising him again Old Trafford tickets as soon as Claire forwards his address, and then a handshake and we are all parted.

I am alone now. How much I have enjoyed their company these past few days. I couldn't have had better travelling companions. It is a strange feeling walking through the airport by myself, having shared so much with the others over the past few days.

Nothing to declare, so straight out of Terminal 3 after ringing the car park firm to be picked up, and after finding the bus stop, wait in the cold drizzle of this English summer's day. An altercation over the road between two cabbies looks as if it could come to blows – where is that friendliness of the Tanzanians twenty-four hours ago? They do eventually give up and drive away with their fares, leaving us to wait longer but eventually our bus arrives, and people in their impatience push through. I'm at the front of the queue with one other guy who has been waiting some time, but others behind push on first, meaning I do get on but for the other guy there is no room and he will have to wait for the next one!

A trip that takes us past the other terminals, and a return to my car park and to pick up my car keys. I load luggage in the boot, then a quick check round for any damage and it's back on the road towards Heathrow to be able to retrace my steps back onto the A4 towards London, the M4 and towards home. As the weather deteriorates, more road works appear as I approach the M4 flyover at Junction 3, strengthening the road, improving the infrastructure for the fast approaching London Games.

Back on the M4, I give Mum and Dad a quick ring, Mum relieved to hear my voice despite knowing my progress. I have a brief conversation with them both, saying I will speak to them later when I have got back home. As I get onto the M40 I also give Graham, who had offered so much encouragement, a ring. He was on my list of people to inform from the summit, so he knew I had done it. We have a long chat about the climb, about my climbing pastures, and about how I felt during and now after the climb, after achieving what has meant so much to me. I think he is quite proud of me for turning my dream into reality, for it was from that chat we had had on the cliffs overlooking Torbay before Christmas, through the training, the walks on the coast with him before going up to Exmoor to do all that walking, he who had been part instigator and part motivator in pushing this project through to completion. The effect on him, will come later.

As I near a motorway services, I realise it has been a long time since I have eaten, so I stop for a cooked breakfast and buy myself a Sunday paper, excitement as the Olympic Torch continues its journey through the country (and I saw it on its second day with Graham and Molly in South Devon), will Murray win Wimbledon? Bradley Wiggins still leads the Tour de France.

Back in the car and up to Birmingham, I have promised myself a decent set of kitchen knives as a reward for achieving what I set out to do, so I stop at Boundary Mill to get these, before completing the journey back to Telford, and home. The day has cleared up and the sun is now shining as I reach my front door.

Quite an adventure as I return to the normality of my life, but something to remember.

I take a quick look around the garden, the vegetables have come on a lot, then it is time to unpack, clothes for washing, the sleeping bag to air, and piles of the equipment I have borrowed to be returned, laid out once again on the lounge floor.

I sift through the post, check e-mails (Dad has sent me one congratulating my success, which for some reason he thought I would pick up on the mountain), and Davina has arrived, more than pleased to see me. I think she was more worried about the climb than she had let on, but I am back safe and sound, full of stories of my trip.

Then we go to the town centre quickly before going to see Dave and Lisa, who have Shirley, his mum, and his sister Sue who I have met before, visiting them. Dave is very excited about the trip and wants to know all about it, wishing he could have done it with me, but he shares in my elation. We chat about Kili for a while, and then on to his wedding plans and how they are progressing. My next adventure, thoughts for the stag weekend, though the wedding is still three months away, but time is flying by.

We must leave, so stop at Frankie and Benny's for a meal to chat more about my adventures and then head home again.

It has been a long day; I have travelled more than a few miles, and now tiredness is catching up with me. Davina stays a while but knowing weariness is overcoming me, leaves me to my home, my thoughts, and my dreams.

I chat again with Mum and Dad on the phone as promised, she is more composed now so we can talk more about Kilimanjaro, the people, and the food, etc.

It is now nine o'clock, and I am tired, very tired so I head for bed. I am home and I have done it. Murray didn't win Wimbledon, but do I care? For despite the fact it is still light, I am in bed and soon asleep, and for once I sleep for a long time....

18. FINALE

And so I have come to the end of my story, well, it's not a story because it is fact. But it would be wrong to finish here, because this has been a lifetime ambition, and because of that, it must have some effect on me.

The following day I intended to be quiet and relaxing because I knew I may be tired and not ready to go back to work, and for the most part, kept myself to myself. I had to finish unpacking, wash clothes, air sleeping bags, liners and other equipment I had borrowed, before returning these items to their owners with a deep gratitude for them lending them to me. I also had to get ready for a return to work, with the changing emotions from achieving something special to going back to the mundane routine of day-to-day life, with the emotions of leaving "my" mountain, the friendship and bond created between the five of us, all of us because I can't forget Chunga, William, and the porters. It was not going to be as easy to go back to reality as it may seem. The day just drifted by, no pressure imposed on myself to get things done, just to be ready for the following day, relax, rest, and be prepared for work. An early night, hopefully to catch up on some of that lost sleep on the mountain.

In actual fact the reception I got from work was fantastic, and I must have repeated the same story several times to different members of staff, who had received the news I had succeeded via the text I had sent James, along with a picture at the summit, and indeed it was on the practice website already as well. The stories about the camera, the climb, altitude sickness, and just how I felt from having done it, everyone was really interested.

I am back at work, and my summer "holiday" is over. But

it would be wrong to finish this tale here, especially as this was at the top of my bucket list, my life time ambitions, and so it must have had some impact on my life.

As I finish this account of my adventure, it is March 2015, nearly three years ago, and if right from the start, I had the intention of writing this, then, it has taken me a long time to get around to it, about a thousand words in two years, but in the past six, seven weeks I have shown the drive that got me to the summit back in 2012.

I had done this climb to raise money for Severn Hospice, secondary to my wish to climb Kilimanjaro, but through the kindness of friends, Serendipity members, and clients and colleagues from work, I did raise a considerable sum for my chosen charity. Through articles I wrote in the Practice newsletter, I was able to show my appreciation to those at work as I gave a quick resume of my climb. At the Serendipity Summer Ball in July 2012, after the main speeches, I was allowed to get up and thank those members who had supported my cause, and thank Margaret especially for her support and encouragement in getting this project off the ground, and helping me achieve my "serendipity" moment. Even guests at the ball I didn't really know stopped me after the meal to talk about the climb, how I felt, how I prepared for it – a lot of interest and esteem was gained from it. And a special personal thank you to Margaret in the bar afterwards, at the end of the day if it hadn't been for her and Graham, then I doubt if I would have done the climb. Also a special mention in my brief speech for Dave Ridgeway, for suggesting the fundraising for the local hospice, and to Jenny for her help in the technical side of the climb, and for dragging me up Snowdon.

Minsterley Show followed in August, where the Practice has a stand, and again in attendance, I was able to thank those who had so kindly supported the cause. Again, I spent much of the day chatting to farmers about my adventure, the trials and tribulations, the walk with a top rugby correspondent, my camera, and would I do it again? It was a long, tiring day but I was happy to relate my tale to those many friends and clients who were interested.

Peake Travel had asked me to go in on my return and tell them of my trip, firstly because they were interested, and secondly to be able to give information to other travellers who may in the future wish to undertake this challenge themselves. Again, my thanks to them for all they did in making the arrangements for me to go, and for it all to happen so smoothly. I cannot praise them enough for sorting it all out, the visa arrangements, and just keeping me up to date with how the arrangements were progressing, because as it turned out, with so few of us signing up to the trip, if it hadn't been for the late booking of Claire and Chris, it may well not have happened.

I have a certificate that says: "This is to certify that Mr Roderick Wood has successfully climbed Mt. Kilimanjaro the Highest in Africa to Uhuru Peak 5895amsl', dated 05/07/2012, Time 6.30 a.m., Age 58. The certificate number is 170529.

Obviously, a lot of other people have done this climb over the years, climbing on different routes, different times of year, and having different motivations for wanting to attempt the climb. Similarly, there are also many who have attempted the climb, but have not succeeded, for whatever reason – fatigue, altitude sickness, whatever. Then there are those who have sadly, as on our summit day, died especially from the effects of altitude. It is far from a formality that one will succeed, and as I found out, at times requires a great deal of self-motivation and drive to reach the top. I do often wonder, since that day, what the certificate number would have been if I had attempted to do this when I first had the ambition, or certainly in my twenties. The great unknown?

But this was my quest, a very personal experience which had its ups and downs, but what effect has it left on me?

Firstly, the mountain still has a great draw for me, especially now I have experienced it first-hand. Any program that features the mountain, newspaper article, anything that has a little snippet about Kilimanjaro, I have to watch or read. I was given for a jigsaw puzzle for Christmas, 1000 pieces, of Kilimanjaro, quite a complex one and very hard, but once I had started it, like the mountain itself, it became compulsive, building the animals, the plains, the ice-covered slopes leading to the summit, all various shades of blue, but like reaching the top of the mountain, the extreme feeling of satisfaction from having completed it was immense, and it lay undisturbed on my dining room table for many weeks. I was loath to break it up again, to pack it away. It's not my mountain, but it has taken a place in my heart, from that feeling I had when Neil and I sat outside after our meal at the Glacier Club, and through the trees in bright sunlight Kilimanjaro looked down on us, to that last long look, up on the steps of the plane, before departing Kilimanjaro Airport to return home.

So, before the effects on me, do I have any regrets about the trip? Regrets, I have a few (there is probably a song there somewhere). A big one would be the loss of my camera, and not being able to record the sights that I wanted to. I am very grateful to Claire for forwarding her pictures to me, but obviously a lot of these photos are personal to her and Chris, and perhaps I missed some that I would have taken that she has not, the mountain streams, me and my tribulations... But, I would have to say that it is nice to have those pictures, especially of the Barranco Valley, where I was not feeling at my best and the part, the most beautiful part, where I was suffering, as I can't recall as clearly as I would like the sights around me. I regret, though I have always been terrible with names, either not knowing or not remembering the names of some of our fantastic porters. I suppose we were never going to keep in contact with them as we went our separate ways, but it would be nice to still be able to put a name to a face.

With that, again, I wish I had taken everyone's e-mail

addresses, as other than Chris, who I have exchanged an odd message now and again, we have sadly lost contact with each other, as Claire never sent on the rest. We formed a great bond on the mountain, as said before, the "if one fails, then we have all failed" attitude – we looked out for each other, laughed at ourselves, we really did get on well together. So I wish that bond had continued. Who knows, one day if I keep trying, I may still get hold of them.

It was a shame not to see any more of the wildlife than the few monkeys, but time did become a limiting factor in the end, and I wouldn't have wanted to have rushed my viewing. So one day I will see them, my elephants, the roaming herds on the Great Rift Valley, the big cats, and hopefully if mankind can control himself, a few rhinos if they can survive. They were what started my love of Africa, so I must see them in their natural state, to me the animals of Africa are a wonder of the world.

The other concern, not a regret but a worry, is the future of the mountain. The three volcanoes, Kilimanjaro, Mawenzi, and Meru all stand out proudly over the African plains. But they are changing. Already, Mawenzi is deemed unsafe to climb because of the fragility of its rock formation, yet it is a striking feature across the alpine desert from Barafu Camp, and indeed on the Rongai route you would walk across this desert and closer to this peak. Meru is sometimes used as an altitude climb before tackling Kilimanjaro, and I am led to believe it is an enjoyable climb over a couple of days, with a greater chance of seeing wildlife. Neither has the height of Kili, and I am afraid I wouldn't know how the climate affects these two peaks in terms of snow. But Kilimanjaro is snow covered, and with glaciers, but how long for? When I reached the summit, it was certainly not as cold as it can get – we were very lucky, with clear visibility all the way. Our walk from Stella Point to Uhuru Peak was through frozen snow, and from the summit as you looked north towards the ice fields and the spectacular dip of the Ash Pit, there was plenty of white to be seen, but between us and the southern ice fields there were areas of bare earth and rock.

The glaciers are still spectacular (especially to one who has never seen a glacier before), and their melt waters were gratefully appreciated by us as our source of drinking water as we climbed the mountain. But, by all accounts, these glaciers are retreating, and doing so quite fast. Over time into our distant past, we have had periods of warmth, and periods of extreme cold where glaciers have been able to grow, and cover more of the summit and upper slopes of the mountain. We can only recall the past century and a bit for this mountain, from the first German explorers to attempt climbing Kili, who would have recorded what they had found, and many of the glaciers would have been named after these explorers. Certainly photographic evidence over the past decades would corroborate this picture of retreat. And to me, I find this is a shame.

There is not a lot we can do to change our climate, but indeed if the retreating glaciers can be attributed to global warming, even at this, the highest point in Africa, then how long can the mountain remain as it is? With more retreat, the rock will become more exposed to the elements, and surely its features will change.

One of my endearing memories will be seeing Kili staring at me from above, between trees, from the steps of the plane, with that snow-covered cap, which to me now is ingrained in my mind as part of an everlasting picture. Even that jigsaw puzzle, those tricky pieces that I struggled with to make the upper slopes and summit. Snow and glaciations to me are a part of Kilimanjaro. If the reduction in the ice continues, how long would it take for them to go entirely? Presumably not that long, even in my lifetime it could occur. That would be very sad. And if there were to be no glaciers, would there be that same attraction of the mountain? For me, I'm not sure. Even for a mountain so close to the Equator, something 5895 metres high should have snow on the top all year round, and glaciers, which is just a personal opinion, but that is the picture painted in my mind of this wonderful piece of nature.

As mankind, we are trying to do something about global warming, and I don't want to enter into the politics (or indeed know enough about it), but if we are trying, will it come quickly enough for Kili? Only time will tell, but that is how I will always remember the mountain, and hope it will be like that for the rest of my life. And longer, so others can enjoy what I have got out of my experience with it, as a child in books, and now having experienced it first-hand. Of course, one mustn't forget the source of income that the mountain brings to a developing country, the number of jobs it creates, and its general effect on the local economy. Talking to Chunga and William, these people have aspirations of their own, and it would be a pity if those were not allowed to develop because of a reduction in the tourist industry.

The other comment I would make about the area, is that although the actual Kilimanjaro National Park covers a large area, the amount of litter one sees is enormous, especially around the campsites. Whether it is the porters, or us the climbers responsible for this blot on the landscape, I don't know. But again, it is a shame that an area of such stunning scenery, diversity, and a great source of local income should be spoilt by people being too lazy to tidy up after themselves. There is also the effect on the local ecosystems, wildlife etc. that this may cause. Some of the campsites would be so much more appealing if some of this litter was collected and disposed of correctly, and may encourage all to be tidier and take care of their own. I gather there are plans to improve sanitary arrangements on the campsites, all can only improve the ambience of the area and encourage everyone to take care of this national treasure.

So in climbing Kilimanjaro, I achieved a lifelong ambition, an arduous holiday but one that I can look back on with pride. I have a bucket list, as previously said – Kili was at the top and I did it. The hot air ballooning over the Nile had been done the previous year, one off. I wanted to be a best man as it would be an indication of true friendship. Dave had got engaged the previous year to Lisa, and it was an honour to be asked to fulfil this task for him in October 2012. The climb was mentioned in my speech, of things I wanted to do and the pride I had in standing by Dave on his big day. A wonderful weekend spent in the Lake District, taking Dave for a walk around Coniston Water in the morning of the wedding to take him away from it all, reflect on life, our friendship and his encouragement for me to reach my goals, and the disappointment that he could not accompany me on my epic journey. His knee probably wouldn't have stood it, but we would have had fun. A weekend when true friendship came through, but my climb still in the background, and giving me a lot of confidence to do my functions, and to make that speech to people I had never met before. Another one done!

White water rafting was on the list, and that was to be the stag do, but sadly due to an accident Dave had, we were not able to do this at the arranged time. But, after a couple of cancellations by the organisers, we did manage on a glorious summer morning in June 2013, to have our go. Setting off early on Dave's bike (a first for me), stopping for a biker's breakfast and then donning our wet suits to raft down the river at Bala, I really found this exhilarating. We had four runs down the river, and I managed to get in the front of the boat for the last three of those runs, so I could hit the white water head on and it was fantastic. Again, a great experience and one I will do again (and in fact have done so in 2015), perhaps somewhere in the future where the water is "wilder". Another one done, which leaves one which may or may not happen, but the effect of the climb on me may make it more likely. Enough on that.

Now two and a half years on, as I reach the conclusion to my story, perhaps it is time to reflect on what it has done for me as a person. Over that time, I have perhaps lost myself as the pace of life has become so hectic, when I should be slowing down, that I have forgotten a bit about me as I have catered for everyone else's needs ahead of my own.

Before I did the climb, I had always enjoyed walking but never done it seriously. I would walk on Exmoor with Dad when I was down there, with Graham in South Devon, taking the dog for a walk, but I had never done any of it seriously. I don't really enjoy climbing hills all that much, but since the Kilimanjaro trip, I have taken more to walking, and by myself, as it gives me some relaxation a chance to enjoy my surroundings, nature, to think and to provide some exercise. I started some road walking that winter of 2012-13, and was then persuaded by Dave and Lisa to join them doing the London Moon Walk in aid of breast cancer in 2013. This involved walking the London Marathon course, but we started at Battersea Power Station as Hyde Park was still recovering from the Olympics. Twenty-six miles and some yards after that, although I'm sure we did more than we were supposed to! I had to train for this; they wanted us to complete the walk averaging some four miles an hour, which is a good pace. So I took to my walking boots again, starting with four to six miles, then gradually upping this to ten, twelve, fourteen, sixteen and finally twenty-one miles walking the Silkin Way through Telford, plus a little more to get up to the required distance. Surprisingly, I actually found this more painful than climbing Kili, and in the end I did find I had to do it at my pace and not Dave and Lisa's, to be able to complete the marathon, so at seventeen miles had to leave them behind me. Walking through and round London, past all the sights, starting at just before midnight and going on past daybreak, was quite an experience, especially as us participating blokes were also encouraged to wear a bra, and Lisa had fitted Dave and I out with a short chiffon skirt, much admired by the ladies as we went on our way. What really surprised me is that London never sleeps – there was a brief lull between four and five o'clock in the morning, then it springs to life again, as one shift (party goers) retires to bed, and the next shift is up and about getting to work. This was a very tiring experience, and the three of us were really dead on our legs when we had completed the event, and then we still had to walk back to the tube station.

On my second anniversary of reaching the summit, I was in Rhodes on holiday, and it was hot, but behind our hotel in Kolymbia was a rocky hill, quite steep, but towering over our bay. I thought that I was going to have to climb this, and chose to do it on that anniversary, purely to celebrate the day of Kili summit, and what it had meant to me. So, in the heat of the afternoon, and with far from ideal footwear, I set off up the sheep track that zigzagged its way up the hill, tricky in places, especially as I neared the top, and in the footwear I had on. The top reached, I was able once again to reflect on the walk of two years previously, and also to enjoy the fantastic views along the eastern coastline of Rhodes, to Rhodes Town in the north, and down to Lindos in the south. It didn't take that long, but it was good to do it to reflect back to that early morning as the sun rose over Uhuru Peak, my achievement, and fulfilment of that life time ambition.

Has it had a lasting effect on me? Has it changed me? I don't have to think long on that question, because it has had a big effect on my life, on me as a person. You meet a surprising number of people who either have just done the climb, who are just contemplating doing it, or have friends, work colleagues, acquaintances who are about to do it, mainly for charity. Many farmers and clients still ask me about the climb, and what I am going to climb next (as if they think I enjoy mountain climbing), and still have a lot of admiration for me doing this, the old codger!

It was only a couple of days ago that I bumped into one of our clients who I had not seen for a while, who was relating to a fellow farmer how I had asked him to sponsor me for the hospice, and him willingly saying yes because there was no way that he thought that I could do it. But as he said, fair dues to me, I stuck at it and got there. Another keeps asking me what my next project is, and then says jokingly that perhaps I should act my age and give up doing these things now (the same one who is fascinated by the number of bands that I go and see in town over a weekend, something I never did when I was younger, and perhaps at an age that I should have done this).

So the prestige, respect, and admiration I have received from the community I have worked in is immense, and not only gives me a topic of conversation with them, but the feel-good factor of that respect and admiration, really puts me on a high. Getting up and speaking in front of 250 of them at our ten-year practice celebration was easy because of the confidence I had got from achieving my goal. Could I have done it before I did the climb? No way!

At times the climb was hard, harder than hard, and it took more than a little determination to push myself on to get to the summit. At times like in the Barranco Valley when I was feeling so rough, the scenery was enough to make me forget how hard I was finding it, to drive myself on, to push up the Barranco Wall, and Claire's encouragement too. But at other times, especially in those early hours of the summit climb out of Barafu Camp, in the middle of the night, when it was monotonous, tiring, boring (queues), and because of the lack of oxygen, it was really hard and took a real determination to keep putting one foot in front of the other, pole, pole, as we slowly ascended towards Stella Point. That was when you really found out about yourself, how far you could push yourself when the going was really tough, but the ambition of a lifetime was so close to achievement. Even Jeff on that final climb, when he really did struggle, and Chunga and two porters, Loderick and Sugar Ray had to help him, many would have turned around then, or be ordered to head back down. But, I would imagine there was no way that he was going to be told that despite feeling so bad, he wasn't going to reach that summit.

The tiredness I felt at Uhuru Peak, the books say that the elation of reaching here far outweighs the tiredness one feels, but having not slept for the duration of the climb, there was no way I could feel that joy – I was knackered. But looking up the following lunchtime from The Glacier Club, that elation did materialise, a sense of achievement, a sense of pride in having pushed oneself to the limit, and beyond, and most of all, fulfilling an ambition. I cannot describe how that felt and still does feel.

So what effect has it had on me? This climb has certainly been the hardest thing I have ever done in my life. The determination it has given me now, in any task that I put my mind to is considerable, just in that inner belief and confidence that I can succeed at something if I really want it. Yes, there were times when I had to be pushed (thank you Margaret), and times of self-doubt in those early months when things were in the planning stage, and just beyond. But once it was in my mind that I could do it (which probably came when doing the Coleridge Way), that determination, some who know me would call it the Wood stubbornness – it was going to happen. The respect for taking on this climb has been immense, though many other people do it and succeed, at my age as well (and one mustn't forget that American amputee we crossed paths with when we were going up, tremendous courage from him, but again I suppose it's something he really wanted).

From my determination to at last do something I had really wanted to do all my life, it gave Graham the drive to do something he had wanted to do for a long time, which was to take himself and Molly off to South Africa, Cape Town, the Garden route, and the Kruger, experiences that will long live with him.

For me now, there is a greater determination to get things done, an idea that I have had at work for many years, to improve the welfare on farms. I have now come up with a template to try and achieve this, and if now out on farms in an embryonic form, at least now it is in motion. This probably has a slight downside now that I do get very frustrated if things don't seem to be happening, or not at the rate I wish them to. Has that made me more intolerant of other people? I don't think so, it is just that desire to be always moving forward.

The holiday was expensive, costing in excess of £3000 in the end, more than I could really afford, but for me as a person, it has been money well spent. The fulfilment of a long-held ambition, the camaraderie that developed between the five of us, and Chunga, William, and the porters, that desire that we were all going to succeed together. The inner belief in myself, and the drive that I now have, all these things will have developed my character to see me through my latter years. It has made me a more rounded person, a more positive person, and a person more relaxed with myself.

And of course, I cannot forget the memories of this adventure, the whole adventure, the walks in Shropshire (of which I will discover more), those lovely walks over Exmoor, seeing the Olympic Torch, a once in a lifetime event in this country. Snowdon from a different view, one I didn't know of, and that wonderful waterfall. The meeting of the group outside Kilimanjaro Airport, and the time we spent together, the pain, the drive, and the scenery around, some more stunning than others, especially that wonderful plant life through the Barranco Valley. The summit, the views of the glaciers, the ice fields, even though shattered at the time, are unforgettable, unique in my humble life; the lasting views of the mountain from the Glacier Club, the plane steps and through the plane window as we left Kili behind us when starting back home. Even the wait at Addis on the return, and our little period of excitement with the mystery bag.

All put together, a highlight of my life. And before this, I would have to admit that I had always hated writing, but even if this only becomes a personal diary for myself, I have really enjoyed putting my thoughts down on paper. Again, it took some time to get started, probably two years to put the first couple of pages down, but over the past few weeks I gained the determination (thank you Jay for the encouragement) to get it done – something to give my grandchildren, and something for me to always go back to, to remind me of this wonderful experience.

So, I can only say to anyone now that if they have a dream, they have to pursue it. The personal benefit is vast, and I would guess that I would always have carried a sense of regret if I hadn't done this. Follow your dreams, succeed in your dreams, and you will find yourself.

So what of the future? I will endeavour to go back to Africa – unfinished business both in meeting those wonderful friendly people in their own country, and especially to do what I missed out on this time round, the great Game Parks, the wildlife, the elephants in their natural surroundings. People ask me what I will climb next, if I don't have a great desire to be running up and down mountains, then if I could combine the wildlife with perhaps Mount Kenya, then that is something else to look forward to. I have put my name down to help in a project to improve the "dairy" industry in Mozambique, and would like to do that as my last act as a vet before I retire, but if that comes off I will have to wait and see (other applicants and the ever-changing face of politics in Africa, all out of my control). It would be nice to give something back to this spectacular continent that I fell in love with so long ago as a child. For sure, I will go back.

The ideas for another book are already in my mind, and I will continue to walk more and discover more of the country that I live in. All positives, and all will bring new and greater experiences to life.

All I can finish with is that if anyone has personal ambitions, then they must try and fulfil them, otherwise they may carry the disappointment of not doing so for the rest of their lives, and the joy it will bring to complete whatever that ambition is, well I can't describe. Do it!

On July 5th I reached the summit of Kilimanjaro, Uhuru Peak, 5895 metres, the roof of Africa. I had succeeded in my ambition of a lifetime. My goal, my fulfilment, and now, my story. One which I will keep with me forever.

And yes, I would do it again!

19. THE LEMOSHO ROUTE

Day 1/2: Overnight flight to Kilimanjaro and travel to Weru Weru River Hotel.

Day 3: Trek from Lemosho Glades to Big Tree Camp. 2780 metres. 3.5 hours.

Day 4: Trek from Big Tree Camp to Shira Camp. 3500 metres. 5 hours.

Day 5: Shira Camp to Northern Ice Fields, camping at Moir Hut. 4175 metres. Walk to Lent Hills (4300 metres) for altitude acclimatisation. 7 hours.

Day 6: Moir Hut to Lava Tower. 4640 metres. Walk to Arrow Glacier (4800 metres) for altitude acclimatisation. 7 hours.

Day 7: Lava Tower to Karanga Valley. 4035 metres. Descent into Barranco Valley before ascending Barranco Wall. 7 hours.

Day 8: Karanga to Barafu Camp. 4640 metres. 2.5 hours.

Day 9: Kilimanjaro ascent to Stella Point (5700 metres), and to the summit, Uhuru Peak (5895 metres), and then descending to Millennium Camp (3790 metres). 14 hours.

Day 10: Millennium Camp to Mweka Gate (1630 metres) and return to Weru Weru River hotel. 3 hours. Party!

Day 11/12: Trip to Moshi, then return flight to Heathrow.

20. EQUIPMENT

High tog sleeping bag (thanks Alex)

Sleeping mat (Alex)

Sleeping bag inner fleece (Roxanne)

Water bottles, four

Hiking Boots – waterproof

Gaiters

Slip on shoes for camp

Socks

Walking socks

Spare laces

Walking trousers

Shorts

Underpants

Long johns

Waterproof overtrousers

Thermal, breathable vests

Long-sleeved polo shirt

Jumper

Fleece

Light windproof jacket

Warm down jacket (Lisa)

Weatherproof overcoat/jacket (Dave)

Thermal gloves (Paul)

Head torch and spare batteries

Basic first aid kit

Wash bag and toiletries

Towel

Sunhat and warm hat

Scarf

Dry bags

Rucksack

Holdall for porters to carry basics to next camp

Sunglasses

Camera (and bring it back with you!)

Pen knife

Ginger biscuits, Kendal Mint Cake

Water sterilisation tablets.

21. ACKNOWLEDGEMENTS

Lastly, it would be wrong not to mention those who had supported me through this adventure.

Graham and Sally, who had encouraged me over the years to have a go at fulfilling my ambition, and Graham and Margaret for giving me the final push to turn dreams into reality – it was you two who finally made me do it.

For those mentioned who lent me various bits of equipment, making it more affordable, thank you all.

To Jenny, for her help, her advice, and taking me up Snowdon.

Mum and Dad for encouragement, and carting me around Exmoor for my practice walks.

To all those that sponsored me, helping me raise money for Severn Hospice.

Frances, at Peake's Travel, for sorting all the arrangements out.

Jayne Weaver for finally pushing, encouraging, me to get this written, and reading it for me. And to Sam Ellis for so much help with wording.

Chunga, William, and all those wonderful and friendly African people, for making the trek so enjoyable, and for all their help.

And of course to Claire, Chris, Jeff, and Neil, fantastic companions for the trip, who made the whole experience so much more memorable, the support we gave each other, and the friendship.

18162180R00117

Printed in Great Britain
by Amazon